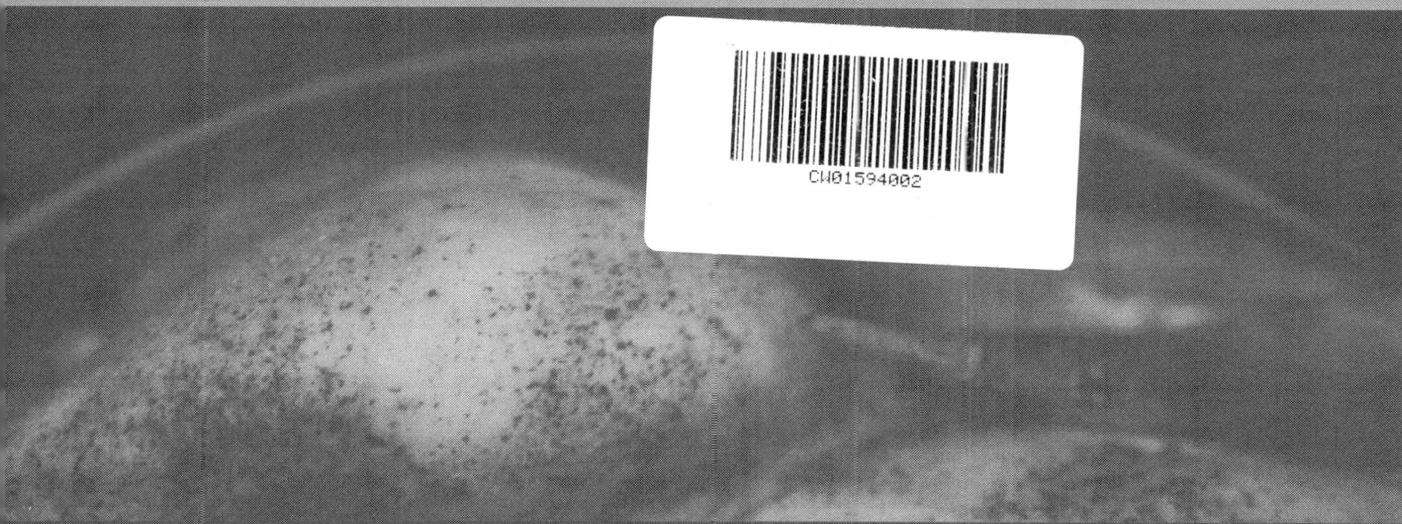



# NINJA FOODI GRILL *Cookbook* 2023

LEARN QUICKLY AND EASILY HOW TO COOK DELICIOUS RECIPES WITH YOUR MULTI-COOKER. IMPRESS YOUR FAMILY AND FRIENDS WITH ORIGINAL TASTES AND EXTRAORDINARY FLAVORS

**Janet McKenzie**

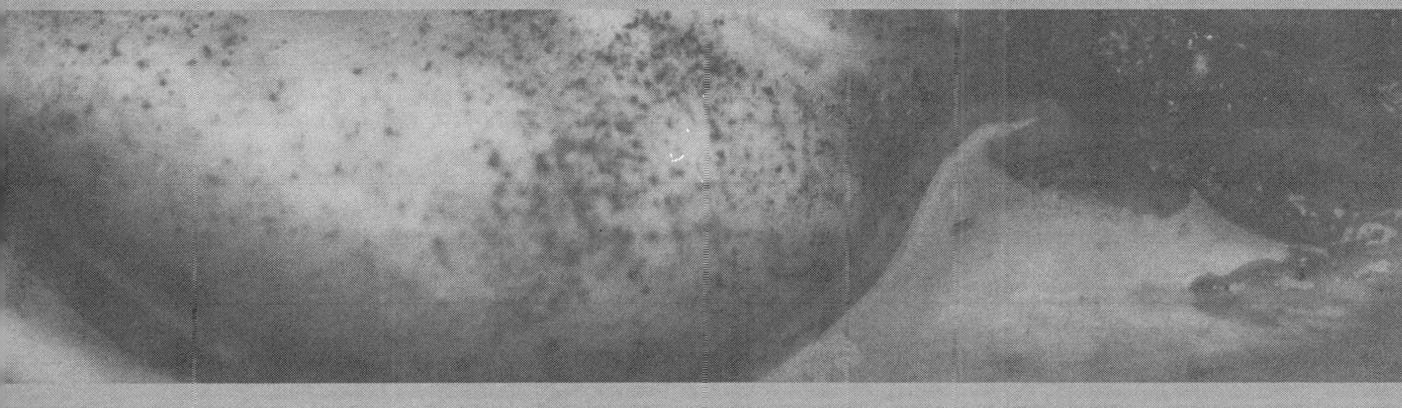

# Table of Contents


**INTRODUCTION** ........ **9**
- What You Need for the Grill ........ 10
- How to Clean the Ninja Foodi Grill ........ 10
- Using the Ninja Foodi Grill ........ 11
- Tips for the Grill ........ 11

**CHAPTER 1 • Easy Breakfast Favorites** ........ **13**
1. Air-Fried Grilled Cheese ........ 14
2. Baked Egg & Bacon-Stuffed Peppers ........ 15
3. Cheese & Chive Scones ........ 17
4. 5-in-1 Grill Air Fryer Omelet ........ 18
5. Grilled Frittata ........ 19
6. Omelet With Potato - Peppers & Cheese ........ 20
7. Simple Zucchini & Egg Muffins ........ 21
8. Cinnamon Rolls With Pecans ........ 23
9. Honey Churros ........ 24
10. Pineapple Toast ........ 25
11. Rose & Honey Grilled Fruits With Baklava Crunch ........ 26

**CHAPTER 2 • Advanced Breakfast Favorites** ........ **27**
12. Garlic Naan for Breakfast ........ 29
13. Grilled Donuts ........ 30
14. Grilled Pizza With Eggs & Greens ........ 31
15. Hungarian Fried Bread ........ 32

**CHAPTER 3 • Easy Vegetarian & Vegan Favorites** ........ **33**
16. Baked Asparagus ........ 34
17. Baked Sweet Potato ........ 35
18. Cajun Eggplant ........ 36
19. Chickpea & Beetroot Koftas ........ 37
20. Grilled Cauliflower Steaks With Greek Salsa ........ 39
21. Grilled Fruit Salad With Honey-Lime Glaze - Vegetarian ........ 40
22. Grilled Harissa Halloumi ........ 41
23. Grilled Watermelon ........ 42

24. Halloumi Pigs in Blankets ....................43
25. Harissa Lentil Veggie Burgers ....................45
26. Ranch-Flavored Cauliflower Steaks....................46
27. Rice & Vegetable Stuffed Peppers.................... 47
28. Rum-Spiked Grilled Mango With Ricotta ....................48
29. Spiced Grilled Grapefruit - Breakfast Specialty ....................49
30. Vegetable Lasagna ....................50
31. Vegetarian Pizza....................51

**CHAPTER 4 • Easy Poultry Favorites ....................53**

32. Air-Crisped Buffalo Chicken Wings.................... 55
33. BBQ Chicken Breasts ....................56
34. Cheesy Chicken Quesadilla Stacks ....................57
35. Chicken Couscous Bowl ....................58
36. Easy Grilled Chicken Thighs....................59
37. Foodi Grilled Juicy Chicken Breasts ....................60
38. Greek Chicken With Tzatziki Sauce ....................61
39. Grilled Chicken Fajitas....................63
40. Grilled Basil Lime Chicken....................64
41. Peri-Peri Grilled Chicken....................65
42. Tandoori Chicken .................... 66
43. Turkey Burger ....................67

**CHAPTER 5 • Intermediate Poultry....................69**

44. Chicken Gyros With Tzatziki ....................70
45. Chicken - Leek - Mushroom & Puff Pastry Pie .................... 71
46. Chicken Roulade With Grilled Vegetables ....................73
47. Chicken Margherita ....................74
48. Chicken Tomatina....................75
49. Hot Fried Chicken ....................76
50. Majestic Alfredo Chicken ....................77
51. Turkey Empanada ....................79

**CHAPTER 6 • Easy Fish & Seafood Favorites....................81**

52. Easy Grilled Shrimp....................83
53. Garlic Salmon Meal....................84
54. Grilled Citrusy Halibut....................85

55. Pil Pil ..........86
56. Salmon Sliders..........87
57. Teriyaki Marinated Salmon ..........89
58. Swordfish With Caper Sauce ..........90

**CHAPTER 7 • Beef Favorites..........91**

59. Bacon-Wrapped Tenderloin Filets .......... 93
60. BBQ Beef Meatloaf .......... 94
61. The Classic Cheeseburgers .......... 95
62. Frikadelle.......... 97
63. Grilled Steak Parmesan .......... 98
64. Pineapple Steak .......... 99

**CHAPTER 8 • Intermediate Beef Favorites..........101**

65. Cool Avocado Steak Salad..........102
66. London Broil..........103
67. New York Strip Steak & Asparagus..........105
68. Pot Roast..........107
69. Steak & Potatoes..........108
70. Steak & Vegetable Kebabs ..........109

**CHAPTER 9 • Lamb - Pork & Other Favorites..........111**

71. Indian Masala Lamb Chops..........113
72. Lamb Kebabs..........114
73. Grilled Ribs ..........115
74. Apple & Sage Pork Tenderloin..........117
75. Juicy Grilled Pork Chops..........118
76. Korean Pork Delight ..........119
77. Chili Dogs ..........121
78. Sausage & Pepper Grinders ..........122

**CHAPTER 10 • Delicious Side Dish & Salad Favorites ..........123**

79. Air-Crisped Sweet Potato Wedges..........124
80. Air-Fried Parmesan Brussel Sprouts..........125
81. Crispy Parmesan Potato Wedges.... ..........126
82. Green Beans Ninja-Style ..........127

83. French Fries With Parmesan & Garlicky Mayo ..... 129
84. Grilled Broccoli ..... 130
85. Honey & Herb Charred Carrots ..... 131
86. Grilled Goat Cheese Crostini With Figs ..... 133
87. Italian Spiced Squash ..... 134
88. Loaded Baked Potato ..... 135
89. Mexican Street Corn ..... 136
90. Rice & Vegetable Stuffed Peppers ..... 137
91. Samosas ..... 139
92. Roasted Red Potatoes ..... 140
93. Stuffed Mushrooms ..... 141
94. Tandoori Cauliflower ..... 142

**CHAPTER 11 • Easy Appetizers & Snacks ..... 143**

95. Air-Crisped Pickle Spears With Special Sauce ..... 144
96. Air-Fried Jalapeno Poppers ..... 145
97. Baked Apple Chips ..... 147
98. Air-Fried Tomato Slices ..... 148
99. BBQ Chicken Egg Rolls ..... 149
100. Beef Liver Pate ..... 151
101. Cheesy Dumplings ..... 152
102. Chili & Cheddar Cheese Zucchini Fries ..... 153
103. Courgette Chips ..... 154
104. Crispy Breaded Asparagus With Creamy Pesto Dip ..... 155
105. Crispy Cheddar Onions ..... 156
106. Curry Chicken Skewers With Mint Dip ..... 157
107. Pigs In a Blanket ..... 159
108. Mozzarella Sticks ..... 160
109. Veggie Egg Rolls ..... 161

**CHAPTER 12 • Advanced Snacks & Appetizers ..... 163**

110. Foodi Grill Air Fryer - Taco Quesadillas ..... 164
111. Granola Bites ..... 165
112. Gnocchi With Walnut & Sage Butter ..... 167
113. Great Mac & Cheese Snack Bowl ..... 168
114. Ham & Cheese Noodle Casserole ..... 169
115. Seared Tuna Salad ..... 170

116. Italian Basil Pizza ........ 171
117. Personal-Size Grilled Pizza ........ 172
118. Pesto & Goat's Cheese Flatbread ........ 173
119. Pizza Snails ........ 175
120. Sea Salt Focaccia ........ 176
**CHAPTER 13 • Dehydrator Favorites ........ 177**
121. Ninja Foodi Spicy Watermelon ........ 178
122. Beef Jerky ........ 179
123. Chicken Jerky ........ 180
124. Dehydrated Apples ........ 181
125. Dehydrated Sweet Potatoes ........ 182
**CHAPTER 14 • Easy Dessert Favorites ........ 183**
126. Caramelized Mango Spears ........ 185
127. Biscoff Brownies ........ 186
128. Lebkuchen Cake ........ 187
129. No-Flour Honey & Peanut Butter Cookies ........ 189
130. Mini Brownies ........ 190
131. Pear Fritters ........ 191
132. Rum Sundae ........ 192
**CHAPTER 15 • Advanced Desserts ........ 193**
133. Apple Strudel ........ 194
134. Beetroot & Tarragon Souffle ........ 195
135. Chocolate Souffle For Two ........ 197
136. Grilled Apple & Raspberry Pie ........ 198
137. Grilled Strawberry Shortcake Skewers ........ 199
138. Persimmon Pomegranate Eton Mess Cake ........ 200
139. Profiteroles ........ 202
140. Quark Schmarrn ........ 205
**CONCLUSION ........ 207**
Benefits of Using the Ninja Foodi ........ 207
Other Tips to Make Grilling Simple ........ 208

# INTRODUCTION

Congratulations on purchasing *Ninja Foodi Grill Cookbook*, and thank you for doing so.

The following chapters will discuss how much the Foodi Grill can help you in the kitchen. It is terrific with its five cooking functions - to grill, to air crisp, bake, roast, and dehydrate.

These are a few of its capabilities.

- Grill: Grill your foods indoors and still have char-grill marks and flavor
- Bake: Use the grill for baked treats, cakes, and much more.
- Roast: The grill will allow you to cook roasted veggies, tender meats, and more using the Ninja Foodi cooking pot.
- Air Crisp: Achieve a crunchy - crispy food with very little or no oil.
- Dehydrate (not included on all models): You can dehydrate fruits, meats, and veggies for healthier snack options. Before dehydrating meats, be sure all fat is trimmed away because fat does not dry out and could cause it to spoil. You will want to finish off the jerky (meat & fish) using the roast function for one minute at 330° F/166° C.

## What You Need for the Grill

The indoor grill comes loaded with many items.

- The grill grate will give your foods that char-grilled appearance. It can fit up to six fish fillets or burgers.
- Air Fry Crisper Basket: You have a four-quart capacity to provide you with two pounds of chicken or fries.
- A Removable Cooking Pot has a six-quart capacity to handle a three-pound roast!
- A splatter shield must always be installed when the grill is in use.

You also have the following:

- 5 Kebab skewers
- Cleaning brush
- Recipe guide
- Quick-start guide

Most of the mentioned items come with the Ninja Foodi Grill package. You may need to purchase the Ninja cooking pot separately.

## How to Clean the Ninja Foodi Grill

1. Start by unplugging the Ninja unit from the electrical outlet.
2. Wipe the central part of the control panel using a clean damp cloth.
3. The cooking pot, grill grate, crisper basket, splatter shield, and other accessories can be washed either by hand or in the dishwasher.
4. If food residue is stuck on the grill grate or crisper basket, place them in a sink filled with warm, soapy water and allow to soak.
5. Air or towel-dry all parts of the Ninja grill after it is cleaned.

# Using the Ninja Foodi Grill

## Warm the Grill

You can get the Ninja® Foodi™ Grill started by selecting the cooking function you'd like and set your timer. You can also adjust temperatures on the display panel as well. Once programmed, the grill will begin to pre-heat. Once you pick your cooking function, temperature, and time, the unit will start to pre-heat. Higher temperatures will take up to approximately eight minutes to heat up. This is a perfect time to assemble ingredients, set the table, or finish cleaning some dirty dishes.

## You have four preset temps for grilling:

- Low Temperature @ 400° F/200° C: Enjoy preparing sausage, bacon, meats with thick sauces or calzones.
- Medium Temperature @ 450° F/230° C: If you need to prepare dinner but have frozen meats, steak tips, and similar items, they can be ready for dinner.
- High Temperature @ 500° F/260° C is excellent for steaks, burgers, chicken, hot dogs, etc.
- Max Temperature @ 510° F/270° C is a plus for pizzas, veggies, fruit, kebabs, fresh and frozen seafood.

# Tips for the Grill

The type of oil used in the grill does matter since it will create less smoke. The pros recommend using oils with a high smoke point, including avocado, canola, coconut, vegetable, or grapeseed oil— instead of olive oil.

The Foodi Grill cooks quickly, so monitor doneness with a food thermometer. Internal food temperature will continue to rise as food rests, so remove it 5° Fahrenheit before the target temperature is reached.

Don't overcrowd the grill. Be sure to evenly arrange and space out ingredients in a single layer to ensure consistent browning and even charring.

Batch Cooking Tips: Empty the fat/oil from the pot's bottom if batch cooking more than twice. For best results, allow the unit to run for three minutes between batches to reheat the grill grate.

You have the basics, so let's get started!

Finally, if you will find this book useful in anyway, a review on Amazon is always appreciated! :)

# CHAPTER 1

# Easy Breakfast Favorites

# Air-Fried Grilled Cheese

TIME REQUIRED
3-5 minutes +
10 minutes per sandwich

SERVINGS
**2 sandwiches**

## INGREDIENTS

- Bread (4 slices)
- Butter/cooking oil spray (1 tbsp.)
- Melted cheese - your preference (1.5 oz./43g)

## DIRECTIONS

1. Place the Ninja crisper basket on the unit and close the lid. Select the air fry function and push the start button to begin the preheat cycle.
2. Make the sandwich with just cheese inside and butter on the outside. Securely close them using toothpicks.
3. Set the timer for three to fiv minutes at 360° F/180° C. Flip the sandwich, slightly increase the heat, and air fry to your liking.
4. Cool before serving and remove the toothpicks.

# Baked Egg & Bacon-Stuffed Peppers

TIME REQUIRED

Under 30 minutes

SERVINGS

**3-4**

## INGREDIENTS

- Cheddar shredded cheese (1 cup)
- Cooked & chopped bacon (4 slices)
- Bell peppers - Seeded - tops removed (4)
- Large eggs (4)
- Fresh black pepper & sea salt (to taste)
- To Garnish: Freshly chopped parsley

## DIRECTIONS

1. Insert the crisper basket and close the hood. Choose the air crisp function at 390° F/200° C for 15 minutes. Hit the start button to start the preheat phase.
2. Separate the cheese and bacon into each of the peppers. Crack an egg in each one and shake a bit of pepper and salt over each one.
3. When you hear the beep, arrange the peppers in the basket and close the hood to cook for 10-15 minutes. The whites should be cooked with a slightly runny yolk.
4. Remove the peppers from the basket, and dust with a bit of parsley to serve.

# Cheese & Chive Scones

TIME REQUIRED

35 minutes

SERVINGS

4

## INGREDIENTS

- Plain flou (9.5 oz./270g)
- Baking powder (0.2 oz./6g)
- Salt (.5 tsp.)
- Chives - finely chopped (1 tbsp.)
- Mature cheddar - grated (1.4 oz./40g)
- Egg (1)
- Unchilled butter - softened (3.5 oz./100g)
- Crème Fraiche (2.1 oz./60g)
- Egg wash: 1 egg + 1 tbsp. milk - for brushing

## DIRECTIONS

1. Sift or whisk the flou with the salt, baking powder, chives, and cheddar into a large mixing container. Whisk and mix in the egg, softened butter, and crème Fraiche. Combine as well as you can, then place on a clean surface and knead only until all loose flou has been worked into the dough.
2. In the Ninja Foodi Grill & Air Fryer, use the cooking pot without the grill plate or crisper basket installed. Close the hood. Choose the bake setting at 340° F/170° C and set the timer to 17 minutes. Press the start button to begin preheating.
3. While the unit is preheating, roll out the dough approximately 0.4 inch/ 3 cm thick. Using a biscuit cutter, cut out scones, rework any leftover dough, and cut again.
4. In a small mixing container, whisk the egg with the milk. Brush the top of the scones with the egg mix.
5. Once the Ninja has preheated, lightly spray the pot with cooking spray and add the scones. Close the lid to begin cooking.
6. When ready, remove the scones and let them cool slightly. Serve with butter, chutney for breakfast, or as a side to soups and stews.

# 5-in-1 Grill Air Fryer Omelet

TIME REQUIRED

11 minutes

SERVINGS

**1**

## INGREDIENTS

- Eggs (2)
- Milk (a splash)
- Vegetables (as desired)
- Shredded cheese (1 handful/as desired)
- Optional: Salt & pepper (as desired)
- Canola oil (as needed)

## DIRECTIONS

1. Whisk two eggs with a splash of milk.
2. Add in the desired vegetables with a handful of shredded cheese, pepper, and salt.
3. Spray the veggie tray with canola oil to avoid food from sticking.
4. Place the tray and air crisper tray in the Ninja grill to preheat.
5. When ready, add in the egg mixture.
6. Cook for 6 minutes at 360° F/180°C.
7. If desired, sprinkle additional shredded cheese at the last minute of cooking.

# Grilled Frittata

TIME REQUIRED

20 minutes

SERVINGS

**8**

## INGREDIENTS

- Eggs (6 large)
- Milk (.25 cup)
- Salt & Pepper (as desired)
- Red & green bell pepper (.25 cup each)
- Mushrooms (4)
- Shredded cheese - your favorite (.5 cup)
- Also Needed: 8.5 inch/ 22 cm round pan
- Canola oil spray: as needed

## DIRECTIONS

1. Dice the peppers and slice the mushrooms.
2. Insert the removable cooking pot and grill grate into the Foodi.
3. Press the *bake* button, set the temperature to 400° F/205° C, and set the timer for ten minutes.
4. Use a large mixing container to whisk the eggs with the salt, pepper, and milk. Add in the peppers, mushrooms, and shredded cheese.
5. Spritz the cake pan with canola spray.
6. Pour the egg mixture into a lightly greased pan.
7. Make a sling using aluminum foil to lay under the cake pan to make it easier to remove.
8. Once the "Add Food" light flashes lay the foil sling on the bottom of the cooker. Lay the cake pan on top.
9. Cook for 12 to 15 minutes until the eggs are set, and the top is a nice golden color.
10. Carefully remove the pan by grabbing the aluminum sling. Wait for fiv minutes before slicing to serve.

# Omelet With Potato - Peppers & Cheese

TIME REQUIRED

35 minutes

SERVINGS

**2**

## INGREDIENTS

- Vegetable oil (0.88 fl oz./ 1 ¾ tbsp.)
- Eggs (6)
- Freshly cracked white pepper & salt (as desired)
- Cheddar cheese - grated (2.63 oz./ 75g)
- Yellow & red bell pepper (½ of each one)
- Onion (1 medium)
- Potatoes (2 medium)
- Button mushrooms (.75 cup/3.5 oz.)
- Baby tomatoes (.75 cup/3.5 oz.)
- Optional: Fresh basil leaves - sliced

## DIRECTIONS

1. Core and dice the peppers. Chop the onions. Dice and parboil the potatoes. Quarter the mushrooms, and slice the tomatoes into halves through the centers.
2. Lightly whisk the eggs with salt, pepper, and about 1.76 oz./ 50g/ 1/3 cup of the cheddar.
3. Ensure the grill plate and crisping basket are removed from the Ninja.
4. Choose the grill function using the med-low temperature setting for 20 minutes. Hit the start button to begin the preheating phase.
5. After it has preheated, open the hood and add the oil to the pot to get hot. Add the onions, close the lid, and cook, stirring regularly until the onions are soft and translucent (5-7 minutes).
6. Add the peppers, close the hood and cook for another three minutes until the peppers have softened slightly. Mix in the potatoes and mushrooms to cook for another three to four minutes, stirring regularly.
7. Pour in the egg and cheese mixture and spread gently around the base of the pan. The egg will start to solidify. Place the sliced tomatoes around the omelet and scatter with the remaining cheese.
8. Close the hood and grill for three to four additional minutes until the cheese starts to turn brown.
9. Sprinkle with the chopped basil and grill one minute before pressing stop to end the cycle.
10. Carefully lift the pan from the grill. Fold the omelet and slice to serve.

# Simple Zucchini & Egg Muffins

TIME REQUIRED

17 minutes

SERVINGS

4

## INGREDIENTS

- Zucchini (1)
- Almond flou (2 tbsp.)
- Butter (1 tsp.)
- Salt (.5 tsp.)
- Whole eggs (4)

## DIRECTIONS

1. Grate and whisk the zucchini with the salt and flour
2. Prepare muffin molds and lightly grease the tins before adding the mixture.
3. Set the Foodi on the air-crisp mode at 375° F/190° C for 7 minutes.
4. Close the hood and bake. Remove and serve when it's nicely browned.

# Cinnamon Rolls With Pecans

TIME REQUIRED

1 hour 55 minutes

SERVINGS

9

## INGREDIENTS

- Plain flou (14 oz./400g)
- Warm milk (7 oz./ 200ml)
- Dry yeast (1.5 oz./43g)
- Sugar (1.4 oz./40g)
- Unchilled softened butter (1.4 oz./40g)
- Egg (1)
- Salt (1 pinch)

**The Filling:**

- Softened butter (1.4 oz./ 40g)
- Brown sugar (1.4 oz./ 40g)
- Pecan nuts - finel chopped (2.45 oz./ 70g)
- Cinnamon (1 tbsp.)

## DIRECTIONS

1. In a medium-sized mixing container, whisk the warm milk with the sugar and yeast. Stir until the yeast and sugar dissolve. Set the bowl in a warm place and allow the yeast to activate (2-3 minutes). Your yeast is activated when the foam starts forming on top of the mixture. Then add butter and egg.
2. Sift the flou with the salt into a large mixing container and pour in the yeast mixture. Thoroughly mix and add the dough onto a floure surface and knead for approximately 2 minutes or until it's completely smooth.
3. Place the dough back in the bowl, cover with a wet tea towel, and leave in a warm place to proof for 1 hour.
4. Once it has doubled in size, place it on a floure surface and roll it into an approximately 14x10 inch/ 35x25 cm rectangle.
5. Brush the dough with melted butter, sprinkle with sugar, cinnamon, and nuts. Tightly roll up the dough starting at the shorter side of the rectangle and carefully slice into 1.2 inch/ 3 cm wide slices. Place the cinnamon rolls on a lightly floure tray and allow to rise for additional 20 minutes.
6. Ensure the pot is installed in the Ninja Foodi Grill & Air Fryer - but the grill plate is removed. Choose the bake setting at 355° F/180° C and set the time to 18 minutes. Choose the start button to begin preheating.
7. Once the unit has beeped, open the hood, lightly spray with baking spray, and add the cinnamon rolls. Make sure you leave at least a 0.4 inch/ 1 cm gap between the rolls as they will expand during cooking. Close the hood to begin cooking.
8. When they are ready, remove the rolls to cool and sprinkle with icing sugar to serve.

# Honey Churros

TIME REQUIRED

20 minutes

SERVINGS

**2**

## INGREDIENTS

- To Coat: Vegetable oil
- Salt (.25 tsp.)
- Water (.5 cup)
- Honey (.25 cup + more to dip)
- Flour (.5 cup)

## DIRECTIONS

1. Ready the Ninja to the air crisper function and set it at 325° F/165° C. Hit the start button to preheat.
2. Prepare the fixing  using the low-temperature setting on the stovetop to create the dough.
3. When the preheat cycle is complete, it will beep, indicating it's ready.
4. Roll the dough into long churro shapes and spritz with a bit of oil.
5. Drop them into the crisper basket, occasionally shaking until browned.
6. Serve with honey for dipping.

# Pineapple Toast

TIME REQUIRED

25 minutes

SERVINGS

4

## INGREDIENTS

- Bread (10 slices)
- Sugar (.25 cup)
- Cooking oil spray (as needed)
- Pineapple slices (10)
- Coconut flake (.5 cup)
- Coconut milk (.25 cup)

## DIRECTIONS

1. Whisk the eggs with the milk and sugar. Add the pineapple slices to soak for about 2 minutes.
2. Warm the Ninja grill by pushing the start button. Set the timer for 15 minutes using the medium setting.
3. Transfer the sliced pineapples to the grill to cook for 2 minutes. Turn them over and cook for another 2 minutes.
4. Continue the process until they are done to serve.

# Rose & Honey Grilled Fruits With Baklava Crunch

TIME REQUIRED

24 minutes

SERVINGS

4

## INGREDIENTS

- Gluten-free oats (.75 cup/2.4 oz.)
- Coconut sugar (1.8 tbsp./0.8 oz.)
- Walnuts (3.5 tbsp./0.8 oz.)
- Ground cinnamon (2 tsp.)
- Ground cardamom (1 tsp.)
- Ground ginger (.5 tsp.)
- Cloves (1/8 tsp.)
- Sea salt (1 pinch/as desired)
- Cubed butter (2.5 tbsp./1.23 oz.)

**The Grilled Fruit:**

- Honey (1 tbsp.)
- Water (1 tbsp.)
- Rosewater (1 tbsp.)
- Zest of 1/2 Orange
- Peaches (2)
- Plums (2)

**The Yogurt Sauce:**

- Greek yogurt (.75 cup/5 oz.)
- The remaining glaze from the grilled fruit

## DIRECTIONS

1. Place the crisper pan into the cooking pot. Choose the air fry function at 300° F/150° C for 5 minutes. Select the start function to begin pre-heating.
2. Meanwhile, combine the dry fixing for the baklava crunch, then add the butter. Rub until the mixture resembles breadcrumbs.
3. Once the unit has preheated, add the baklava crunch mix to the crisper pan and spread it out. Close the hood and cook until the halfway mark. Open and give the mixture a stir and resume cooking.
4. Combine the honey with the water, rosewater, and orange zest into a small bowl to create a glaze.
5. When the unit has completed cooking, remove the cooking pot, lift out the crisper pan, and leave it to cool.
6. Place the cooking pot back into the unit, insert the grill plate, and close the hood. Select the grill setting at the max temperature for 6 minutes.
7. Hit the start/stop button to begin pre-heating.
8. When the unit beeps and displays the 'ADD FOOD' prompt, glaze the fla side of the fruits and arrange them face down onto the grill plate. Glaze the tops, then close the hood.

# CHAPTER 2

## Advanced Breakfast Favorites

# Garlic Naan for Breakfast

TIME REQUIRED
5 minutes

SERVINGS
**4**

## INGREDIENTS

- Self-rising flou (6.65 oz./1.5 cups)
- Plain Greek yogurt (7 oz./0.8 cup/200 g)
- Salt (1 pinch)

**The Garlic Butter:**

- Butter (.33 cup/2.63 oz.)
- Garlic - crushed (2 cloves)

## DIRECTIONS

1. Combine the dough fixing in a mixing container, mixing thoroughly with your hands to shape it into a ball. Split it into two to four balls. Use your hands to spread the dough into the desired shape.
2. Add the air fryer basket and hit start to preheat the unit.
3. Spray each side of the naan with olive oil and set the timer for 5 minutes at 375° F/190° C.
4. Flip halfway through the cooking process and serve.

# Grilled Donuts

TIME REQUIRED

30 minutes

SERVINGS

8 donuts + rounds (if desired)

## INGREDIENTS

- Whole milk (.25 cup)
- Vanilla extract (1 tsp.)
- Powdered sugar (2 cups)
- Prepared biscuit dough (16 oz. tube/ 450g)
- Cooking spray (as needed)

**Toppings: As Desired:**

- Mini marshmallows
- Crumbled cookies
- Rainbow or chocolate sprinkles
- Cinnamon sugar
- Also Needed: 1 inch/ 2.5 cm ring mold

## DIRECTIONS

1. Whisk the milk with the powdered sugar and vanilla extract to create a sugar glaze, and set it to the side for now.
2. Lay the biscuit dough on a fla work surface, such as a cutting board.
3. Use the mold to cut a hole in the center of each round of dough, placing them onto a plate. Pop them into the fridge to chill for 5 minutes.
4. Note: Make donut holes from the cut-out centers.
5. Install the grill grate in the unit and close the hood. Choose the start/stop function for preheating.
6. Select Grill, using the medium-temperature setting for 6 minutes. After 5 minutes, transfer the dough rounds from the fridge and spritz them using a cooking oil spray (both sides).
7. When the unit beeps to indicate it has preheated, place the four rounds on the grill grate. Close the hood and cook for 3 minutes.
8. Remove the donuts from the unit using rubber-tipped tongs.
9. Arrange the last four rounds onto the grill and close the hood to cook for 3 minutes.
10. When ready, remove the donuts from the grill to cool for 5 minutes.
11. When they are cooled to handle, dunk one side of each in the sugar glaze.
12. Arrange the prepared donuts on a platter, glaze-side up, and sprinkle with toppings as desired. Serve promptly for the best flavo results.

# Grilled Pizza With Eggs & Greens

TIME REQUIRED

Under 30 minutes

SERVINGS

**1-2**

## INGREDIENTS

- All-purpose flou (2 tbsp./as needed)
- Pizza dough (½ of a store-bought pizza/8 oz./ 225g)
- Canola oil - divided (1 tbsp.)
- Ricotta cheese - fresh (1 cup)
- Eggs (4 large)
- Fresh black pepper & sea salt
- Torn arugula (4 cups)
- E-V olive oil (1 tbsp.)
- Lemon juice (1 tsp. - freshly squeezed)
- Grated parmesan cheese (2 tbsp.)

## DIRECTIONS

1. Insert the Ninja grill grate and close the lid. Choose the grill setting set to max temperature for 7 minutes. Begin preheating by pushing the start button.
2. Meanwhile, generously dust the countertop/cutting board with flou to roll out the 9 inch/ 23 cm round until it's even.
3. Lightly brush the dough with oil (½ tbsp.), fli the dough to the second side and add the rest of the oil. Use a fork to poke fiv or six holes into dough to help reduce bubble pockets during baking.
4. When you hear the beep, add the dough to the heated grate, close the lid and cook for 4 minutes. At that time, fli it over and spoon the ricotta cheese - leaving a 1 inch/ 2.5 cm border.
5. Crack an egg in a ramekin to keep the yolk intact. Pour an egg into each quarter of the prepared dough. Sprinkle with some pepper and salt. Close the hood and cook the rest of its time (3-4 minutes) until the egg whites are firml cooked.
6. In the meantime, toss the oil with the arugula, juice, and a bit of salt and pepper as desired.
7. When ready, place the pizza on a cutting board to cool. Top it off with the mixture of arugula with a spritz of oil and a sprinkle of cheese.
8. Slice and serve!
9. Note: If you prefer scrambled eggs, just scramble and cook them before placing them on the dough to serve.

# Hungarian Fried Bread

TIME REQUIRED
2 hours 40 minutes @
1 ½ hours of prep time

SERVINGS
**8**

## INGREDIENTS

- Potatoes (5.25 oz./150g)
- Warm water (5.25 fl oz./ 150 ml)
- Warm milk (2.63 fl oz./75 ml)
- Fresh yeast (0.7 oz./20g)
- Sugar (.5 tsp.)
- Salt (.5 tsp.)
- Strong plain flou (13.2 oz./375g)
- Shallot (1)
- Bacon (5 strips)
- Sour cream (3.5 oz./100g)
- Dash white pepper & garlic salt (1 dash each)
- Dried parsley (.25 tsp.)
- For Brushing: Rapeseed oil
- Also Needed: Stand mixer fitte with a dough hook
- Optional: Nutty grated cheese - ex. - Gouda or Swiss

## DIRECTIONS

1. Thoroughly rinse and peel the potatoes. Boil them in salted water. Mash them with a fork and set aside.
2. Pour in the milk and warm water and crumble the yeast into the mixer bowl. Stir in the sugar and let sit until bubbly (5 minutes).
3. Sift in the salt and flour Knead on the low setting until the dough pulls away from the sides.
4. Mix in the mashed potatoes to knead until the dough forms a smooth ball (approx. 5-10 minutes).
5. Using your hands, form the dough onto a floure surface and shape it into a round ball. Lightly oil the bowl and place the ball in the bowl to proof.
6. Use a piece of plastic wrap to cover the container. Let the yeast work until it has doubled in size (1 hour).
7. Meanwhile, fry and chop the bacon and shallot, adding them to a mixing container with the sour cream, white pepper, garlic salt, and parsley. Adjust the seasoning as desired and cover the mixture. Put it into the fridge for now to chill.
8. When the dough is ready, use oiled hands to push it down and remove it from the bowl. Use a knife to divide it into eight portions. Flatten each piece with your hand into a thinner circle in the center and thicker on the edges. Let the prepared dough rest under a tea towel.
9. Insert the crisper basket on the Ninja unit. Choose the air fryer setting at 410° F/210° C for 5 minutes. Select the start button to begin preheating.
10. When the unit beeps, it has preheated. Spray or brush the crisper basket with some oil, then add one to two portions of dough.
11. Brush the tops of the dough with a little oil. Close the hood and air fry for 5 minutes.
12. When cooking is complete, use silicone tongs to remove the langos from the crisper basket to a warming plate.
13. Continue the cooking process until all the dough has been air fried. When all the langos are ready, serve promptly with the sour cream sauce. If desired – you may also sprinkle with a portion of cheese.

# CHAPTER 3

## Easy Vegetarian & Vegan Favorites

# Baked Asparagus

TIME REQUIRED

6 minutes

SERVINGS

**4**

## INGREDIENTS

- Asparagus (1 bunch)
- Olive oil (as needed)
- Sprinkle garlic granules (to taste)
- Salt & pepper (to taste)

## DIRECTIONS

1. Add the air fryer basket to the Ninja Foodi grill & Air fryer AG301.
2. Rinse and pat the asparagus dry. Break off the woody end parts. Brush the grates with a little oil. Add the asparagus to the basket of the fryer.
3. Sprinkle the asparagus using garlic granules, and season as desired.
4. Set the temperature at 390° F/200°C for 5 minutes. Flip them over at the halfway marker.
5. Remove from the Ninja and serve.

# Baked Sweet Potato

TIME REQUIRED

37 minutes

SERVINGS

4

## INGREDIENTS

- Sweet potatoes (4)
- Salt (as desired)
- Olive oil (2 tbsp.)

## DIRECTIONS

1. These are amazingly light and fluffy sweet potatoes with the perfect crispy skin.
   Rub olive oil and salt on the outside of each sweet potato.
2. Put the air fryer basket inside the Ninja. Set the temp to 390° F/200° C for 35 minutes, checking at the ½-hour marker.
3. Remove immediately, slice, flu the middle, and add toppings as desired, such as butter.

# Cajun Eggplant

TIME REQUIRED

22 minutes

SERVINGS

4

## INGREDIENTS

- Olive oil (.25 cup)
- Eggplants (2 small)
- Cajun seasoning (3 tsp.)
- Lime juice (2 tbsp.)

## DIRECTIONS

1. Slice the eggplants and coat them with the oil, juice, and cajun seasoning.
2. Select the grill function on medium for 10 minutes. Push the start button to preheat.
3. When it beeps, arrange the prepared slices over the grate, close the hood and cook for 10 minutes.
4. Flip them over for the fina 5 minutes and serve.

# Chickpea & Beetroot Koftas

TIME REQUIRED

20 minutes

SERVINGS

**2**

## INGREDIENTS

- Chickpeas (7 oz./200g)
- Pickled beetroot (1.4 oz./40g)
- Shallot (1)
- Vegan breadcrumbs (0.7 oz./20g)
- Garlic (1 clove)
- Cinnamon (.25 tsp.)
- Cayenne pepper (.5 tsp.)
- Cumin (.25 tsp.)
- Coriander (1 tsp.)
- Salt and pepper (as desired)
- Cooking spray (as needed)

## DIRECTIONS

1. Drain the chickpeas and beetroot. Dice the shallot and cloves. Chop the coriander.
2. Place all of the fixing into a blender. Blend until well combined but with small chunks still present.
3. Insert the grill plate into the Ninja unit and close the hood. Choose the grilling function set on high for 10 minutes. Push in the start button to preheat.
4. Meanwhile, divide the chickpea mix into four equal parts and form into mini loaves around the skewers.
5. Once the unit has preheated, spray the grill plate using a spritz of cooking spray and add the koftas. Close the hood to begin cooking.
6. After 5 minutes, fli the koftas to make grill marks on both sides. Close the top to continue cooking.
7. Serve promptly with salad or grilled vegetables.

# Grilled Cauliflower Steaks With Greek Salsa

TIME REQUIRED

47-50 minutes

SERVINGS

2

## INGREDIENTS

- Cauliflowe (1 head)
- Kalamata olives (.33 cup)
- Roasted red peppers (.5 cup)
- Fresh oregano (1 tbsp.)
- Garlic (3 peeled cloves)
- Fresh parsley (1 tbsp.)
- Juice of 1 lemon
- Feta cheese (.5 lb./8 oz./ 230g)
- Kosher salt, as desired
- Ground black pepper (1 tsp.)
- Walnuts (.33 cup)
- Red onion (1 small)
- Canola oil - divided (.25 cup)

## DIRECTIONS

1. Do the prep. Remove the pits from the olives and chop. Mince the garlic, parsley, and oregano. Chop the red peppers and onions. Juice the lemon and roughly chop the walnuts. Crumble the feta.
2. Remove the stem and leaves from the cauliflower Slice it from top to bottom into two 2 inch/ 5 cm. "steaks." Reserve the remaining cauliflower**
3. Make the Greek salsa. Toss the olives, oregano, parsley, roasted red peppers, garlic, lemon juice, salt, pepper, feta, walnuts, red onion, and two tablespoons of oil.
4. Insert the grill grate in the Ninja unit and close the lid. Choose the grill function, set the temperature to "max," and set the time for 17 minutes. Hit the start button to begin preheating.
5. While the unit is preheating, brush the remaining oil (2 tbsp.) on both sides of "steaks," sprinkling each one using salt, as desired.
6. Once you hear the beep, it has preheated. Arrange the steaks on the grill grate. Close the hood and set the timer for 10 minutes.
7. At that time, fli the "steaks." Close the hood and continue cooking for another 5 minutes.
8. Now, spread the "steaks" generously with the salsa. Close the lid and cook for the last 2 minutes. Reserve the remaining Greek salsa.
9. When cooking is complete, serve promptly.
10. ** Slice the remaining cauliflowe into large chunks, toss with canola oil, and grill for 12 minutes before tossing with remaining Greek salsa.

# Grilled Fruit Salad With Honey-Lime Glaze - Vegetarian

TIME REQUIRED

Under 30 minutes

SERVINGS

**2-3**

## INGREDIENTS

- Strawberries (.5 lb./8 oz./ 230g)
- Pineapple chunks (9 oz. can/ 250g)
- Peaches (2)
- Honey - divided (6 tbsp.)
- Freshly squeezed limes (1 tbsp. juice)

## DIRECTIONS

1. Rinse, remove the hull, and slice the strawberries into halves. Drain the pineapples and reserve the juice. Remove the pits from the peaches and slice them.
2. Insert the grill grate and close the lid. Choose the grill setting on max for 4 minutes. Hit the start button to preheat the grill.
3. In the meantime, toss the pineapple, peaches, and berries with three tablespoons of honey.
4. After the Ninja buzzes, the preheat is done. Arrange the fruit, gently pressing for the gill indentions. Securely close the hood and grill for 4 minutes - not turning them.
5. Whisk one tablespoon of the pineapple juice with the lime juice and the rest of the honey (3 tbsp.).
6. After the cooking cycle is done, add the fruit to a large bowl with the honey mixture, and serve promptly. It's delicious with bananas, mango, and watermelon too!

# Grilled Harissa Halloumi

TIME REQUIRED

4 minutes

SERVINGS

4

## INGREDIENTS

- Harissa (4 tbsp.)
- Zaatar (2 tsp.)
- Olive oil (2 tbsp.)
- Halloumi (15.75 oz./ 450g)

## DIRECTIONS

1. Insert the grill plate into the cooking pot of the Ninja unit and close the hood. Choose the *grilling function* at max for 4 minutes.
2. Whisk the harissa paste with the zaatar and olive oil. Drain the halloumi and pat dry with a kitchen towel. Cut approx. 16 cubes of halloumi, and toss the halloumi in the harissa paste mixture until evenly coated.
3. After the Foodi has preheated and the 'add food' prompt comes up on the screen, place the halloumi onto the grill and close the hood.
4. Flip after 2 minutes of cooking using silicone tongs.
5. Serve promptly with salad, in a pita/ wrap, or a sandwich.

# Grilled Watermelon

TIME REQUIRED

7 minutes

SERVINGS

**4**

## INGREDIENTS

- Watermelon (6 slices @ 2.9 inch/ 7.5 cm)
- White sugar (1 tbsp.)

## DIRECTIONS

1. Insert the grill plate into the Foodi Air Grill and Fryer and close the hood. Choose the grill function set to “max” for 2 minutes. Push the start button to begin preheating.
2. Season the watermelon slices liberally on both sides with sugar.
3. When the unit beeps, arrange the watermelon on the grill plate. Press down gently to increase contact with the grate. Close the hood and grill for 2 minutes without flipping
4. When it’s ready, serve promptly.
5. Add two teaspoons chili powder and the zest of one lime to the sugar before seasoning the fruit for a change of pace to ‘kick’ it off

# Halloumi Pigs in Blankets

TIME REQUIRED

33 minutes

SERVINGS

6

## INGREDIENTS

- Aubergine (1 small)
- Juice of ½ lemon
- Melted coconut/avocado oil (2 tbsp.)
- Sea salt (1 pinch)
- Halloumi cheese (8 oz. block/ 225g)
- Tamari sauce or soy sauce (1 tbsp.)
- Maple syrup or Agave nectar (1 tbsp.)
- Optional: Liquid smoke (1 tsp. to 1 tbsp./as desired)
- Thyme leaves (1 tsp.)
- Zest of 1 lemon
- White pepper (as desired)

## DIRECTIONS

1. Start by placing the grill plate into the removable cooking pot of your Ninja Foodi Grill and Air Fryer. Set the unit to 'max' for 4 minutes.
2. While waiting, slice the aubergine lengthways into six 0.2 inch/ 0.5 cm slices (by hand or using a mandoline). Whisk the lemon juice with one teaspoon of oil and sea salt, then brush both the front and back of each slice of aubergine.
3. Wait for the preheated buzz. Add the slices to the grill and fli halfway through cooking using a pair of silicone tongs. Remove and repeat if necessary.
4. Slice the halloumi into six 'chip' shaped chunks, and set to one side. Whisk the remaining oil and the rest of the ingredients into a mixing container. Brush the glaze over a piece of aubergine and wrap around one piece of halloumi. Repeat until all of the halloumi is wrapped.
5. Remove the grill plate and add the crisper basket. Place each aubergine-wrapped halloumi piece into the basket. Use the air-fry setting at 340° F/170° C for 8 minutes.
6. Flip halfway through and serve promptly after cooking for the full time.

# Harissa Lentil Veggie Burgers

TIME REQUIRED

28 minutes

SERVINGS

4

## INGREDIENTS

- Brown lentils - well-drained (14 oz. can/ 400g)
- Rapeseed oil, divided (2 tbsp.)
- Tomato paste (2 tbsp.)
- Harissa paste (1 tsp.)
- Carrots (2.63 oz. or 2 medium/75g)
- Spring onions (2)
- Parsley (.53 oz./half of 1 bunch/ 15g)
- Coriander (.53 oz./half of 1 bunch/ 15g)
- Ras el Hanout (1.5 tsp.)
- Panko crumbs (2.63 oz./ 75g)
- Salt & pepper (as desired)

## DIRECTIONS

1. Do the prep by draining the lentils. Peel and coarsely grate the carrots. Finely chop the onions, parsley, and coriander.
2. Place three-quarters of the drained lentils into a food processor container with one tablespoon of oil, the tomato paste, and harissa paste. Process it to a smooth paste.
3. Toss the remainder of the lentils in a bowl with the processed paste and all remaining ingredients (apart from the remaining oil). Season them to taste.
4. Wait for about 5 minutes for the panko crumbs to absorb some of the moisture.
5. Shape the mixture into four balls and pat out into roughly 4.35 inch/ 11 cm burgers.
6. Insert the grill plate in the Ninja unit and close the top. Choose the grill function set to high for 8 minutes. Begin preheating by pushing the start button.
7. Meanwhile, brush the patties on both sides with the rest of the oil.
8. Once the unit has beeped and preheated, place the four burgers on the grill plate and close the lid.
9. After 4 minutes, open the hood and fli the burgers. Close the hood to finis cooking.
10. Serve the burgers in warmed pita pockets with grilled red peppers, rocket, salad, tahini, garlic, and lemon sauce. Or just enjoy it on a traditional burger bun or brioche bun with tomato, cucumber, lettuce, and smoky or spicy ketchup.

# Ranch-Flavored Cauliflower Steaks

TIME REQUIRED

25 minutes

SERVINGS

**4**

## INGREDIENTS

- Cauliflowe  (1 head)
- Canola oil (.25 cup)
- Shredded cheddar cheese (1 cup)
- Pepper & salt (as desired)
- Paprika (.5 tsp.)
- Garlic powder (.5 tsp.)

To Garnish:

- Ranch dressing
- Cooked bacon (4 crumbled slices)
- Freshly chopped chives (2 tbsp.)

## DIRECTIONS

1. Remove the leaves and stem from the cauliflower  Slice it from top to bottom, making 2 inch/ 5 cm 'steaks.' Reserve the rest of it.
2. Whisk the oil with the paprika, garlic powder, pepper, and salt. Brush the steaks on both sides.
3. Set the foodi to max using the grill function for 15 minutes. Push the start button to preheat.
4. When it beeps, place the steaks on the grate and close the hood for 10 minutes.
5. Flip them over and top with the cheese. Close the lid and cook for 5 additional minutes.
6. When ready, drizzle with the dressing, chopped chives, and bacon to serve.

# Rice & Vegetable Stuffed Peppers

TIME REQUIRED

50 minutes

SERVINGS

6 peppers

## INGREDIENTS

- Red or green bell peppers (6)
- Garlic (4 minced cloves)
- White onion, peeled, diced (1 small)
- Instant rice - cooked in the microwave (2 @ 8.5 oz. bags/ 2 @ 250g)
- Red enchilada sauce (10 oz. can/ 280g)
- Fajita spice mix (1 oz./ 28g)
- Diced green chilis - drained (4 oz. can/ 110g)
- Vegetable stock (.5 cup)
- Shredded Colby Jack cheese - divided (8 oz./ 230g)

## DIRECTIONS

1. Prepare the peppers. Chop the top 0.5 inch/ 1.2 cm sections and reserve. Discard the seeds and ribs. Chop the 0.5 inch/ 1.2 cm portions and toss them into a large mixing container. Toss the remainder of the fixing to the mixing bowl, except whole bell peppers and half the cheese.
2. Use the cooking pot without the grill grate or crisper basket installed. Close the hood. Select the roasting function at 350°F/180° C (32 min.). Choose the start mode to begin preheating.
3. Meanwhile, spoon and pack the prepared mixture into the peppers, fillin them up as full as possible.
4. When the unit beeps, arrange the fille peppers, standing upright in the pot. Securely close the hood and continue cooking for 30 minutes.
5. At that point, sprinkle the rest of the cheese over the top of the peppers. Close the lid and continue cooking for the last 2 minutes.
6. When cooking is complete, serve them promptly for the best flavo results.

# Rum-Spiked Grilled Mango With Ricotta

TIME REQUIRED

2 hours 20 minutes

SERVINGS

**2**

## INGREDIENTS

- Water (4.38 fl  oz./125 ml)
- Agave nectar (3 tbsp.)
- Vanilla powder (.5 tsp.)
- Cardamom pods (12 crushed)
- Red Leg Spiced Pineapple Rum/your favorite (2.1 fl oz./60 ml)
- Sea salt (1 pinch)
- Ripe mangoes (2)
- Coconut oil - melted (1 tsp.)
- Shelled pistachios (0.88 oz./25g)
- Ricotta cheese (7 oz./200g)

## DIRECTIONS

1. Prepare a saucepan with the water, vanilla powder, agave nectar, and cardamom pods using the medium-temperature heat setting. Boil, stirring until everything comes together. Adjust the temperature and simmer for 3 minutes. Transfer the pan to a cool burner and mix in the rum and salt. Thoroughly cool it.
2. Once the syrup has cooled, cut the mangoes vertically down the mango's length - roughly 1/4 inch/ 0.6 cm from the stem.
3. Repeat on the opposite side. You should have two flesh 'cheeks.' Place one cheek, skin side down, on a chopping board and score a criss-cross pattern into the flesh  being sure not to cut the skin beneath.
4. Place the mango fles   side down into a shallow container and pour over the syrup allowing it to soak into the cracks. Turn the mangoes over, then leave to marinate in the fridge for 2 to 6 hours.
5. Place the pistachios in a dry pan and roast using the low-temperature setting until lightly browned and fragrant. Transfer to the countertop to cool for a few minutes before roughly chopping.
6. Remove the mangoes from the fridge and transfer the syrup to a small pan.
7. Insert the grill plate into the Ninja unit and choose "grill at max" for 6 minutes.
8. Meanwhile, allow the syrup to come to a low boil, occasionally stirring. Remove the syrup from the stove once thickened and reduced (6-8 min.).
9. When the unit beeps, open and brush the grill plate with a small portion of coconut oil. Arrange the mango's fles   side down and close the hood. When it's ready, transfer to a plate with silicone tongs.
10. Leave the mangoes to cool for a few minutes before turning inside out and place onto serving plates.
11. Serve with ricotta, the reduced syrup, and chopped pistachios as desired.

# Spiced Grilled Grapefruit - Breakfast Specialty

TIME REQUIRED

9 minutes

SERVINGS

4

## INGREDIENTS

- Ruby grapefruits (2)
- Ground cinnamon (1 tsp.)
- Raw cane sugar (2 tbsp.)
- Ground cardamom (.25 tsp.)
- Sea salt (1 pinch)

## DIRECTIONS

1. Place the grill plate and set the Ninja Grill & Air Fryer to the grill setting using the high setting for 7 minutes and let the unit pre-heat.
2. Slice the grapefruits in half and sprinkle the sugar over the tops.
3. Whisk and evenly sprinkle all the spices, followed by a pinch of sea salt on each.
4. Once the unit prompts to "add food," carefully arrange each grapefruit half, cut side down on the grill. Close the unit and leave to cook for the allocated time.
5. Once cooking is complete, remove using a pair of silicone tongs and serve immediately.

# Vegetable Lasagna

TIME REQUIRED

1 hour 10 minutes

SERVINGS

**9**

## INGREDIENTS

- Dried lasagne pasta sheets (1 pack)
- Olive oil (2 tbsp.)
- Courgette (1)
- Broccoli (5 oz./140g)
- Red and yellow bell pepper (1 of each)
- Champignon mushrooms (5 oz./ 140g)
- Tomato passata (18 oz./500g)
- Water (3.5 oz./100 ml)
- Garlic cloves (2 minced)
- Oregano (1 tsp.)
- Rosemary (.5 tsp.)
- Basil (1 tsp.)
- Thyme (.5 tsp.)
- Pepper and salt (to your liking)
- The Cheese Layer:
- Hard cheese - grated (5 oz./ 140g)
- Mozzarella - grated (5 oz./140g)
- Heavy cream (8.75 fl oz./250 ml)
- Nutmeg (1 pinch)
- Salt & pepper (as desired)

## DIRECTIONS

1. Thoroughly whisk the olive oil with 14 oz./ 400g of tomato passata, garlic, oregano, basil, thyme, rosemary, salt, and pepper in a large mixing container.
2. Chop and add the vegetables to the tomato sauce and stir well.
3. Combine the hard cheese with the mozzarella, heavy cream, nutmeg, salt, and pepper in a mixing container.
4. Combine the rest of the tomato passata with water. Spread out half of the mixture on the cooking pot's bottom.
5. Cover the bottom of the cooking pot with lasagne sheets and spread on ¼ of vegetable mixture evenly. Layer with more pasta sheets and then spread 1/3 cheese mix. Repeat this until you have used all the vegetable and cheese mix.
6. For the fina layer, top the lasagne with the remaining tomato water mix. Cover with a layer of baking paper and aluminum foil to prevent it from drying out during baking.
7. Arrange the pot with lasagne in the unit. Choose the bake setting at 340° F/170° C for 45 minutes. Push the start button to begin preheating.
8. Once the unit has beeped to show it has preheated, open, and add the dish. Close the hood to begin cooking.
9. When cooking has completed, remove the pot from the unit and wait about 10 minutes.
10. Serve hot with freshly grated parmesan and basil.

# Vegetarian Pizza

TIME REQUIRED

15 minutes

SERVINGS

**1**

## INGREDIENTS

**The Passata Mix:**

- Crushed garlic cloves (2)
- A pinch of dried oregano
- Salt and pepper (as desired)

**The Pizza:**

- Olive oil (2 tbsp.)
- Pre-made pizza dough (1 pack)
- Mushrooms (3)
- Jalapeno slices (1 tbsp.)
- Red pepper (1/4 of 1)
- Corn kernels (2 tbsp.)
- Red onion (1/2 of 1 small)
- Mozzarella and cheddar (combined - 2 handfuls)

## DIRECTIONS

1. Finely chop the mushrooms and onions, and slice the jalapenos. Cut the peppers into 1 inch/ 2.5 cm squares.
2. Combine the fixing for the passata mix in a mixing container. Preheat the grill on the bake setting, using the high-temperature setting.
3. Lightly flou a working surface. Roll out the pizza dough and poke holes all over with a toothpick.
4. Once the grill has preheated, place the dough into the grill and allow it to bake on high for 3 to 4 minutes.
5. Open the grill and carefully add the passata and vegetables to the dough.
6. Top with the cheese. Bake until the cheese has melted (4-5 min.).
7. Serve as a delicious snack or lunch.

# CHAPTER 4

## Easy Poultry Favorites

# Air-Crisped Buffalo Chicken Wings

TIME REQUIRED

36 minutes

SERVINGS

4

## INGREDIENTS

- Chicken wings (2 lb./ 900g)
- Canola oil (2 tbsp.)
- Prepared buffal sauce (.5 cup + more as desired)

## DIRECTIONS

1. Rinse and pat dry the wings. Toss them into a large mixing bowl with the oil until evenly coated.
2. Insert the crisper basket in the unit and set it to air crisp at 390° F/ 200° C. Set the timer for 26 minutes. Begin the preheat cycle using the start/stop function.
3. It will beep once it's preheated. Arrange the wings in the basket, evenly spread them out, close the hood, and set the timer to cook for 12 minutes.
4. Stir the wings with rubber-tipped tongs and close the hood to continue cooking for 12 more minutes.
5. At that time, remove wings from the basket. If you want them crispier, you can continue to cook for an additional minute.
6. Transfer the wings to a large mixing bowl. Mix them with the buffal sauce using rubber-tipped tongs. Serve and enjoy them immediately.

# BBQ Chicken Breasts

TIME REQUIRED

38-40 minutes

SERVINGS

**4**

## INGREDIENTS

- Frozen boneless, skinless chicken breasts (4 @ 8 oz./ 55g each)
- Canola oil - divided (2 tbsp.)
- Kosher salt (as desired)
- Ground black pepper & salt (to taste)
- A favorite barbecue sauce (1 cup)

## DIRECTIONS

1. Place the grill grate in the Ninja unit and close the hood. Select the grill mode to the medium-temperature setting for 25 minutes. Click the start button to preheat.
2. Meanwhile, brush the chicken with ½ tablespoon of oil. Sprinkle the salt and pepper over the chicken to your liking.
3. When you hear the beep, it's preheated, so you can arrange the chicken on the grill grate. Close the Foodi hood and set the timer for 10 minutes.
4. At that time, turn the chicken and close the lid to cook for an additional 5 minutes. Then, generously baste the breasts using the barbecue sauce (both sides). Close the hood and continue cooking for 5 more minutes.
5. Thoroughly baste the chicken and cook for 2 minutes. If it's not done at that point, baste it, and continue cooking until the centermost part reaches 165° F/75° C (internal temp.).
6. Wait for 5 minutes before serving.
7. Cooking Tip: If using a thicker barbecue sauce, grill using the low setting instead of medium.

# Cheesy Chicken Quesadilla Stacks

TIME REQUIRED

40 minutes

SERVINGS

**4**

## INGREDIENTS

- Flour tortillas (4)
- Salsa (2.8 oz./80g)
- Hot sauce (3-5 drops)
- Sour cream (2.8 oz./ 80g)
- Chopped grilled chicken breast - divided (12 oz. - approx/ 350g)
- Spring onions (5 - chopped - divided)
- Diced jalapeño peppers - divided (3.5 oz. can/ 100g)
- Grated cheddar - divided (18 oz. + 2 oz./ 480g + 60g)
- Cheese (17.5 oz./ 500g)
- Cooking oil spray (as needed)

## DIRECTIONS

1. Insert the grill plate onto the Ninja unit and close the hood. Choose the grill function with it set to max temperature for 4 minutes. Select the start button to begin preheating
2. Meanwhile, spray both sides of the tortillas with cooking spray. Poke five to seven small holes in each tortilla to prevent them from ballooning during the cooking process.
3. Whisk the salsa with the sour cream and hot sauce; set aside.
4. When the unit beeps, place one tortilla on the grill plate. Close the hood and grill for 1 minute. Next, open the lid and remove the tortilla; set aside. Repeat with the remaining three tortillas
5. Spread a grilled tortilla with a third of the chopped chicken, a third of the spring onions, a third of the jalapeño peppers, 6 oz./ 160g cheese, and a third of the salsa mixture. Place another tortilla on top.
6. Top that tortilla with 1/3 of the chopped chicken, 1/3 of the spring onions, 1/3 of the jalapeño peppers, 6 oz./ 160g cheese, and 1/3 of the salsa mixture.
7. Place another tortilla on top. Continue to layer after placing the last tortilla on top, press down gently.
8. Remove the grill plate from the unit. Choose the roast function and set the temperature at 360° F/180° C. Set the timer for 23 minutes. Push the start button to begin preheating.
9. When the unit beeps to signify it has preheated, place the tortilla stack in the pot. Cover it with an aluminum foil tent, pressing down gently to secure foil around the stack. Close the hood and cook for 20 minutes.
10. At that point, remove the foil. Sprinkle the rest of the cheese over the top, close the hood, and continue cooking for the remaining 3 minutes.
11. When cooking is complete, remove it with a non-metal spatula, transfer to plate, slice, stack, and serve.

# Chicken Couscous Bowl

TIME REQUIRED

25 minutes

SERVINGS

**2**

## INGREDIENTS

- Water (4.2 fl oz./120 ml)
- Vegetable stock (.5 cube)
- Couscous (4.2 oz./120g)
- Chicken breasts (2 sliced)
- Oil (1 tbsp.)
- Paprika (1 tsp.)
- Salt & black pepper (as desired)
- Garlic powder (1 tsp.)
- Bell pepper (1)
- Onion (1)
- Tomatoes (2 diced)
- Sriracha sauce (1 tbsp.)
- Tomato puree (2 tbsp.)
- To garnish Feta cheese and parsley

## DIRECTIONS

1. Deseed and dice the bell pepper. Peel and dice the onion and tomatoes.
2. Boil 0.5 cup/120 ml of water and add the vegetable stock cube to it. Stir until the stock is dissolved. Add the couscous into a bowl and pour the stock over it. Cover the bowl and set it to the side.
3. Be sure the pot is installed but the grill plate is removed.
4. Choose the roasting function set at 390° F/ 200° C for 15 minutes. Punch in the start button to begin preheating.
5. Toss the chicken with the oil, salt, paprika, garlic powder, and pepper.
6. Once the unit has beeped to signify it has preheated, add the seasoned chicken, and close the hood to begin cooking.
7. When 10 minutes are left on the timer, open the hood. Add in the bell pepper, onion, and tomatoes. Close the top to continue cooking.
8. At the 3-minute mark, mix in the Sriracha, tomato puree, and the prepared couscous.
9. Before serving, stir in parsley and a garnish of feta cheese. Serve hot.

# Easy Grilled Chicken Thighs

TIME REQUIRED

20 minutes

SERVINGS

**8**

## INGREDIENTS

- Chicken thighs (3 lb./ 1.4kg)
- Meat tenderizer - ex McCormick (as desired)

## DIRECTIONS

1. Warm the grill using the medium-temperature setting, making sure the grill plate is installed before preheating.
2. Trim the bones from the chicken and season the thighs using the desired tenderizer.
3. If needed, cook the chicken in batches - in a single layer. Grill them for 7 minutes.
4. Flip the chicken and grill side two until thoroughly cooked, tender, and juicy for 7 minutes.
5. Use a meat thermometer to check for doneness (170° F/80° C).
6. Serve with your favorite side dish.

# Foodi Grilled Juicy Chicken Breasts

TIME REQUIRED

1 hours and 15 minutes

SERVINGS

**4**

## INGREDIENTS

- Chicken breasts (4)
- Balsamic vinegar (2 tbsp.)
- Soy sauce (3 tbsp.)
- Worcestershire sauce (1 tbsp.)
- Brown sugar (.25 cup)
- Olive oil (1/3 cup)
- Minced garlic (3 tsp.)
- Pepper and salt (as desired)

## DIRECTIONS

1. Whisk the oil with the balsamic vinegar, soy sauce, salt, pepper, brown sugar, Worcestershire, and minced garlic. Set aside ¼ cup for serving.
2. If the breasts are thick, put each piece between sheets of plastic wrap and beat until even and thin.
3. Poke each of the breasts with a fork forming pockets. Put the chicken into the marinade to work for at least 20 minutes.
4. Insert the grill grate into the cooker.
5. Press the grill button and set the temperature to medium for 25 minutes.
6. When the preheater buzzes, add the chicken onto the grill and put the hood back down to cook for 8 to 10 minutes. Open the grill and fli the meat, closing the grill once again. Cook for another 5 minutes, open the hood and baste the chicken with more of the marinade.
7. Cover and cook for an additional 5 minutes. Check the internal temp to ensure you do not overcook it (165° F/75° C).
8. Flip the chicken one last time and baste it. Cook as long as needed until you reach the correct internal temp.
9. Wait for about 5 minutes before cutting it to serve.

# Greek Chicken With Tzatziki Sauce

TIME REQUIRED
25 minutes

SERVINGS
4

## INGREDIENTS

**For the Breasts:**

- Chicken breasts (4)
- Olive oil (.25 cup)
- Dried oregano (2 tsp.)
- Lemon juice (1 medium lemon)
- Sea salt & freshly cracked pepper (as desired)
- Garlic powder (1 tsp.)

**For the Sauce:**

- Finely grated cucumber (.5 cup)
- Apple cider vinegar (2 tsp.)
- Greek yogurt/sour cream (1 cup)
- Juice of one medium lemon
- Garlic powder (1 tbsp.) or Garlic cloves (1-2 minced)

## DIRECTIONS

1. Whisk the lemon juice with the olive oil, salt, oregano, pepper, and garlic powder in a medium mixing container. Pour it into a zipper-type baggie/container with the chicken to marinate in the fridge for a minimum of 2 hours.
2. Prepare the tzatziki sauce by firs grating the cucumbers. Squeeze all of the excess cucumber juice out of the shreds before mixing with the remaining ingredients.
3. Mix in the vinegar, Greek yogurt, lemon juice, garlic, and sea salt in a mixing container. Chill in the refrigerator until it's time to serve.
4. Warm the Ninja Foodi grill to 400°F/200° C and add the marinated chicken.
5. Prepare the chicken breasts for about 5 to 7 minutes per side, depending on thickness. Transfer them from the grill and wait a few minutes before slicing.
6. Slice the chicken over a bed of rice or stuff into a pita. Top with the creamy tzatziki sauce and a lemon wedge on the side.

# Grilled Chicken Fajitas

TIME REQUIRED

30 minutes

SERVINGS

**6**

## INGREDIENTS

- Red/Green/Orange or Yellow bell pepper (3 total @ 1 each for color)
- Sweet onion (.5 cup)
- Chicken breast (6)
- Fajita seasoning (2 tbsp.) or Store-Bought - Gluten-Free/Regular (1 Packet/to taste)
- Corn/Flour tortillas
- Canola/Olive oil cooking spray

## DIRECTIONS

1. Use the grill grate that comes with the Ninja Foodi Grill and prepare it using the high-temperature setting to preheat.
2. Trim the chicken, removing all skin and bones.
3. Once the Foodi prompts you to 'add food,' carefully spritz the inside of the cooker using a bit of cooking oil spray. Dice and add in the onion, peppers, and chicken.
4. Top it off with the seasoning. Spray them with cooking spray.
5. Grill for 20 minutes on high, turning the chicken midway at 10 minutes.
6. Once the cycle is complete, check the temperature; it needs to be at least 165° F/75° C - internally.
7. Once it is thoroughly cooked, carefully remove and serve on warm tortillas.

# Grilled Basil Lime Chicken

TIME REQUIRED

1 hour 14 minutes

SERVINGS

**5**

## INGREDIENTS

**The Marinade:**

- Chicken thighs (3 lb./ 1.4kg)
- Black pepper & salt (as desired)
- Soy sauce (3 tbsp.)
- Dijon mustard (3 tbsp.)
- Worcestershire sauce (3 tbsp.)
- Limes (2 - juiced & zested)
- Olive oil (3 tbsp.)
- Green onions chopped (3)
- Garlic (2 cloves)

**Dressing Ingredients:**

- Extra virgin olive oil (.25 cup)
- Lime juice and zest (1)
- Cloves of garlic (2)
- Green onions (3)
- Basil (2 tbsp.)

## DIRECTIONS

1. Chop the basil, onions, garlic, and peppers.
2. Combine the marinade fixing in a baggie or container. Add the chicken to marinate for a minimum of 1 hour to overnight.
3. Preheat the Ninja grill using the medium-temperature setting.
4. Trim the chicken to remove all of the bones and fatty skin.
5. Grill (in batches if needed) for 7 minutes per side or until the chicken reaches at least 170° F/80° C. Wait about 3 minutes before cutting.
6. In the meantime, whisk the dressing fixing in a mixing container.
7. Slice the chicken into bite-sized pieces. Serve with a portion of dressing over the top.

# Peri-Peri Grilled Chicken

TIME REQUIRED

30 minutes

SERVINGS

4

## INGREDIENTS

**The Chicken:**

- Chicken legs (4 whole - skin on)

**The Marinade:**

- Juice of 1/2 lemon or lime
- Crushed garlic (3 cloves)
- Salt (1 pinch)

**The Peri-Peri Sauce:**

- Red pepper (¼ of 1) or fier red chilies (1-2)
- Cayenne pepper (.25-.5 tsp.)
- Garlic (2 cloves)
- Lemon or lime juice (1.7 oz./ 48g)
- Smoked paprika (2 tbsp.)
- Olive oil (1.7 oz./ 48g)

**The Garlic Bread:**

- French baguettes (2)
- Olive oil (4 tbsp. + as needed)
- Crushed garlic (2 cloves)
- Salt (1 pinch)
- Oregano (2 tsp.)

## DIRECTIONS

1. Prepare the marinade mix by mincing and whisking the garlic with the lime and salt. Dump it over the chicken. Cover and let it marinate for 1 hour.
2. Insert the grill plate into the Ninja Foodi Grill and Air Fryer and close the hood. Turn the grill function to the high setting for 30 minutes. Hit the start button. Once the Ninja beeps, it means it's a perfect temperature.
3. Sprinkle the chicken with a bit of salt and arrange it skin side down onto the grill, closing the hood.
4. Check it at the 10-minute marker. If the skin has grill marks, turn it over. If not, cook for a few more minutes and then fli it, close the top, and cook for another 10 minutes.
5. Brush both sides with the Peri-Peri sauce and cook for another 5 minutes, turning over halfway through the cycle.
6. Take a piece of chicken out and, with the point of a sharp knife prick into the chicken near the joint to check if it's thoroughly cooked. Then let it rest on a warmed plate as you make the garlic bread.
7. Set the grill using the medium setting for 6 minutes. Whisk the oil with the oregano and garlic.
8. Slice the bread lengthwise and then dip into the herbed garlic oil. Arrange it on the grill and cook for 3 to 5 minutes and serve.

# Tandoori Chicken

TIME REQUIRED

55 minutes

SERVINGS

**6**

## INGREDIENTS

- Chicken thighs or legs (32 oz./ 2 lb./ 900g)
- Plain yogurt (4.4 oz./125 g)
- Garlic cloves (4-6)
- Ginger (1 inch/ 2.5 cm piece)
- Kashmiri chili powder (1 tbsp.)
- Tandoori paste or powder (2 tbsp.)
- Coriander powder (1.5 tsp.)
- Salt (as desired)
- Garam masala (1 tsp.)
- Turmeric (0.5 tsp.)
- Cumin powder (1 tsp.)
- Lemon juice (1 tbsp.)
- Ghee/oil (2 tbsp.)

## DIRECTIONS

1. Slice two large slits into each chicken thigh/leg. Crush the ginger and garlic.
2. Toss all of the fixing with the chicken in a large mixing container. Rub the marinade into the meat. Allow the chicken to marinate for a minimum of ½ hour or up to 24 hours.
3. Insert the grill plate into the Ninja Grill and close the hood.
4. Use the grill function setting the temperature to the highest option for 18 minutes. Spray with oil and add the chicken to the grill plate.
5. Flip the chicken midway through cooking and baste. Check that the chicken is cooked through fully before removing it. Place it back on the grill for a few more minutes if required.
6. Serve with naan or rice (optional).

# Turkey Burger

TIME REQUIRED

50 minutes

SERVINGS

**4**

## INGREDIENTS

- Burger buns (6 - sliced into halves)
- Ground lean turkey (2 lb./ 900g)
- Plain granola (3 oz./ 85g)
- Red onion (1 large)
- Feta cheese (1 cup)
- Salt (.25 tsp.)
- Black pepper (.5 tsp.)
- Sun-dried tomatoes (2/3 cup)

## DIRECTIONS

1. Chop the tomatoes and onion. Crumble the feta.
2. Whisk all of the fixing in a mixing container to make six patties.
3. Set the Foodi grill for 14 minutes in the medium setting. Preheat the grill by pushing the start button. Wait for the beep.
4. Arrange the patties on the grate and cook for 7 minutes.
5. Flip them over and continue cooking until they are done to serve as desired.

# CHAPTER 5

# Intermediate Poultry

# Chicken Gyros With Tzatziki

TIME REQUIRED

35 minutes

SERVINGS

2 gyros

## INGREDIENTS

**Make enough marinade for 3 pieces:**

- Vegetable oil (.5 cup)
- Minced garlic (2 cloves)
- Red wine vinegar (.25 cup)
- Mixed herbs - dill, basil, cilantro, etc. (.5 cup)
- Lemon juice (.5 tbsp.)
- Mustard (1 tsp.)
- Pepper & salt (as desired)

**The Tzatziki:**

- Minced garlic (2-3 cloves)
- Plain greek yogurt
- Dried grated cucumber
- Dill
- White wine vinegar
- Lemon juice
- Olive oil
- Pepper & salt (to taste)

**The Gyros:**

- Flatbread (2 pitas)
- Chicken breast fillets (1)
- Beef tomato (1 sliced)
- Sliced cucumber (half of 1)
- Red onion (1 sliced)
- Crumbled feta (.25 cup)

## DIRECTIONS

1. Combine all of the marinade fixings in a zipper-type freezer bag. Marinate the chicken in the bag overnight.
2. Make the tzatziki by combining all of the fixings except the salt, lemon juice, oil, and pepper in a mixing container. Sprinkle in the salt to taste.
3. Squeeze in the juice and a drizzle of oil. Let it chill in the fridge for at least ½ hour.
4. Make the gyros by placing the grill grate in the Foodi unit. Close the hood and select the grill setting on high for 14 minutes. Push the start button and preheat the cooker.
5. When it beeps, grill the fillets until they are no longer pink (10-14 min.).
6. Slice them into strips and assemble the pitas with the cucumbers, chicken, tomatoes, feta, and red onion. Serve with a drizzle of tzatziki over the top.

# Chicken - Leek - Mushroom & Puff Pastry Pie

TIME REQUIRED

65 minutes

SERVINGS

4

## INGREDIENTS

- Light olive oil (2 tbsp.)
- Chicken thighs (10.5 oz./ 300g)
- Chunky smoked bacon or pancetta lardons (2.1 oz./60g)
- Chestnut mushrooms (10.5 oz./300g)
- Leek (1 large - cut into 0.6 inch/ 1.5 cm slices)
- Thyme - leaves picked (4 sprigs)
- Ready-made béchamel/white sauce (9.7 fl oz./275 ml)
- Dijon mustard (2 tsp.)
- Chives (1.5 tsp.)
- Flat parsley (1.5 tsp.)
- Tarragon (1.5 tsp.)
- All-butter puff pastry (preferably in a block) kept fridge cold (7 oz./200g)
- Egg (1 yolk)
- Black pepper & salt (as desired)

## DIRECTIONS

1. Chop the parsley, chives, and tarragon; set aside for now.
2. Trim the bones and fat from the chicken and slice them into chunks. Slice the mushrooms in half and quarter if needed.
3. Place the chicken, lardons, mushrooms, leeks, salt, pepper, and thyme in a bowl with the oil.
4. Ensure that the grill plate and crisping basket are removed from the pot. Select the roast function, set the temperature to 375° F/ 190° C for 15 minutes. Select the start button to begin preheating.
5. When the unit beeps to signify it has preheated, add the contents of the bowl into the pot and give it a quick stir around to spread it out evenly. Close the hood to begin cooking.
6. Open the lid and give it a stir after about 8 minutes. Close the hood and continue cooking. Check again after 12 minutes to see if it's done, or give it another stir and continue cooking.
7. When it's done, remove the pot from the unit and scoop all the contents along with their juices into a bowl. Wash the pot and return to the unit.
8. Add the béchamel sauce, mustard, and chopped herbs to the chicken mix. Taste and adjust seasoning if necessary.
9. Cool the mixture to room temperature before proceeding or chill for later use.
10. When ready to bake the pie, place the fillin in a 8 inch/ 20 cm pie tin or dish about 1.6 inch/ 4 cm deep.
11. Roll the puff pastry into a 9 inch/ 23 cm circle just under 0.2 inch/ 0.5 cm thick. Return the pastry to the fridge for about 15 minutes to chill and rest.
12. Make an egg wash by mixing the yolk with 1.5 teaspoons of water and a small pinch of salt.
13. Brush the egg wash onto the lip of the pie dish to help the pastry stick to it. Place the puff pastry circle over the fillin and press all around the edge with the prongs of a fork. Brush the pastry all over with the remaining egg wash, and then prick the top of the pie a few times with the fork.
14. Choose the bake function 375° F/190° C for 25 minutes. Push the start button to begin preheating.
15. When the unit beeps, carefully pop the pie into the pot and close the hood.
16. After 10 minutes, reduce temperature to 340° F/170° C and continue cooking
17. When cooking is complete, carefully lift the pie out of the pot and serve it piping hot.

# Chicken Roulade With Grilled Vegetables

TIME REQUIRED

45 minutes

SERVINGS

4

## INGREDIENTS

- Chicken breasts (4)
- Ham (4 slices)
- Grated parmesan (1.4 oz./40g)
- Fresh parsley & basil (1 tbsp. each)
- Courgette (1)
- Yellow and red bell pepper (1 each)
- Garlic (1 clove - minced)
- Black pepper and salt (as desired)
- Oregano (1 tsp.)
- Olive oil (1 tbsp.)

## DIRECTIONS

1. Finely chop the basil and parsley. Halve and quarter the courgette. Slice the peppers into 0.6 inch/ 1.5 cm pieces.
2. Start by cleaning the chicken breast and butterflyin them open. Lightly pound them using a meat mallet until thin. Sprinkle the entire surface of the chicken with pepper and salt. Sprinkle one side with parmesan, and then place 1 slice of ham on each chicken breast. Sprinkle them using freshly chopped herbs and roll them up. Secure each of the ends with toothpicks.
3. Insert the grill plate in the Ninja unit and close the hood. Choose the grill function, setting the temperature to medium for 25 minutes. Push the start/stop button to begin preheating.
4. Meanwhile in a large bowl, toss the courgette, bell peppers, oregano, garlic, salt, pepper, and olive oil.
5. Wait for the beep to signify the grill has preheated. Gently arrange the chicken rolls on the grill plate and close the hood to begin cooking.
   When 10 minutes are left on the timer, open the lid, and add vegetables. Close top to continue.
6. When ready, remove chicken rolls and wait for about 2 minutes. Serve them piping hot.

# Chicken Margherita

TIME REQUIRED

27 minutes

SERVINGS

**8**

## INGREDIENTS

- Garlic cloves (6 minced)
- Balsamic vinegar (1.5 cups)
- Vegetable oil. (4 tbsp.)
- Freshly chopped basil (.5 cup)
- Rosemary, cilantro, & pepper (.25 tsp. each)
- Salt (.5 tsp.)
- Chicken breast fillets (8)
- Mozzarella cheese (8 slices)
- Tomatoes (2 diced)

## DIRECTIONS

1. Whisk the oil with the vinegar, seasoning, and cloves to prep the marinade.
2. Add the chicken to marinate for ½ hour.
3. Arrange the Ninja grill in the unit and close the hood. Select the grill function for 15 minutes using the high setting. Choose the start button to preheat.
4. When you hear the beep, add the chicken to the grill for 6 minutes.
5. Close the hood and wait. When ready, top it off with basil, cheese, and tomatoes.
6. Close the lid and continue cooking for another 5 to 10 minutes until the chicken is a nice golden brown. Serve promptly.

# Chicken Tomatina

TIME REQUIRED

22 minutes

SERVINGS

4

## INGREDIENTS

- Garlic (1 clove)
- Salt (.5 tsp.)
- Olive oil (2 tbsp.)
- Vinegar (.75 cup)
- Fresh basil leaves (.25 cup)
- Plum tomatoes (8)
- Chicken breast (4)

## DIRECTIONS

1. Mince the garlic. Trim the chicken and remove the skin and bones.
2. Measure and add the oil, salt, garlic, basil, and vinegar into a food processor, pulsing until it's smooth. Add the tomatoes and mix again.
3. Use a mixing container and combine the marinade with the chicken to chill in the fridge for 1 to 2 hours.
4. Set the Foodi grill to the high setting for 6 minutes. Push the start button to begin preheating. After you hear the beep, place the chicken on the grate to cook for 3 minutes. Turn it over and cook for the fina 3 minutes before serving.

# Hot Fried Chicken

TIME REQUIRED
48 minutes +
marinate time (8 hours)

SERVINGS
**3-4**

## INGREDIENTS

- Black pepper (1 tbsp.)
- Mustard powder (1 tbsp.)

**Spices @ 2 tbsp. each:**

- Garlic powder
- Chili powder
- Kosher salt
- Onion powder
- Buttermilk (1 quart/4 cups)
- Uncooked chicken thighs (2)
- Uncooked chicken breasts (2 - each split in half)
- Canola oil - divided (.75 cup)
- Dark brown sugar (2 tbsp.)
- Cayenne pepper (2 tsp.)
- Paprika (3 tbsp.)
- All-purpose flou (4 cups)

## DIRECTIONS

1. Leave the chicken and bones in the chicken.
2. Whisk the salt, pepper, garlic, onion, chili, and mustard powders. Place half the mixture in a large zipper-type plastic bag or container.
3. Combine the buttermilk with the spice mixture. Set aside the remaining spice mixture.
4. Toss the chicken with the buttermilk mixture and marinate in the fridge for 8 hours or overnight.
5. Time to Cook: Strain the chicken from the marinade. Combine the rest of the spice rub with flou in a big mixing container. Working in batches, dip the chicken pieces in the flou mixture until evenly coated. Gently shake the chicken to remove excess flour
6. Insert the crisper basket in the Ninja unit and close the hood. Select the air crisp function at 360° F/ 180° C for 25 minutes. Start the preheat cycle by pushing the start button.
7. Meanwhile, rub each piece of chicken with oil, using a total of ¼ cup oil for all pieces.
8. When the unit beeps, arrange the chicken in the basket. Close the hood and cook for 10 minutes.
9. Whisk the rest of the oil (½ cup) with the paprika, brown sugar, and cayenne pepper in a mixing container.
10. After 10 minutes, turn the chicken and close the lid to cook for another 10 minutes, then check the chicken for doneness. Continue cooking up to an additional 5 minutes or until the chicken's internal temperature reaches 165° Fahrenheit/75° Celsius.
11. When cooking is complete, gently toss chicken with the spiced oil mixture and serve.

# Majestic Alfredo Chicken

TIME REQUIRED

30 minutes

SERVINGS

4

## INGREDIENTS

- Halved chicken breasts (4)
- Chicken seasoning (4 tsp.)
- Provolone cheese (4 slices)
- Crumbled blue cheese (.25 cup)
- Alfredo sauce (.5 cup)
- Lemon juice (1 tbsp.)
- Apple (1 large in wedges)

## DIRECTIONS

1. Prepare a medium container with the chicken along with the seasoning.
2. Toss the apple and lemon juice into another container.
3. Set the Foodi grill at 16 minutes using the medium mode.
4. Once it beeps, add the pieces of chicken to the grate and cook for 8 minutes.
5. Flip them over and close the hood to continue cooking for the fina 8 minutes.
6. Place the apple on the grill and cook for 4 minutes (two per side).
7. Serve the deliciously grilled chicken with the apple, blue cheese, and alfredo sauce.

# Turkey Empanada

TIME REQUIRED

55 minutes

SERVINGS

**6**

## INGREDIENTS

**The Dough:**

- Butter in cubes (.25 cup)
- Flour (1.5 cups)
- Cold water (.25 cup)

**The Filling:**

- Canned/boiled small potatoes (1 cup - cubed)
- Medium onion (1)
- Frozen peas (.25 cup)
- Salt (.5 tsp.)
- Chili powder (1 tsp.)
- Ground turkey (6 oz./ 170g)
- Vegetable oil (2 tbsp. + more for frying)
- Tomato paste (1 tbsp.)
- Freshly chopped parsley (1 tbsp.)
- Also Needed: Processor with a blade attachment

**Optional Toppings:**

- Sour cream
- Salsa
- Favorite dip

## DIRECTIONS

1. Make the dough. Combine the butter, salt, and flou in the processor. Mix in the cold water and egg to create the dough ball.
2. Form a fla disk. Wrap it in plastic wrap and pop it in the fridge for at least 1 hour to overnight.
3. Prepare the fillin by warming a large skillet using the med-high temperature setting. Add the oil and onion to sauté until it's translucent. Mix in the turkey and sauté for another 4 to 5 minutes before adding the tomato paste to cook for another 2 minutes.
4. Cool slightly and add the rest of the fixings
5. Place the crisper basket on the Foodi and close the hood. Preset the heat by hitting the start button and air fry mode.
6. Roll the dough and cut into circles. Fill the with ¼ cup of fillin and crimp the edges with a fork after folding into halves.
7. Wait for the buzzer, and lightly spray them with the oil and fry in batches of three for 2 to 3 minutes or until nicely browned.
8. Serve as desired.

# CHAPTER 6

## Easy Fish & Seafood Favorites

# Easy Grilled Shrimp

TIME REQUIRED

10 minutes

SERVINGS

8

## INGREDIENTS

- Jumbo raw shrimp - deveined - shell on (2 lb./ 900g)
- Canola/Olive oil (2 tbsp.)
- Seasoned salt - ex. - Lawry's (1 tbsp.)
- Old Bay Seasoning (1 tbsp.)

## DIRECTIONS

1. Warm the grill using the medium to medium-high temperature setting.
2. Combine each of the fixing in a mixing bowl or gallon-sized baggie.
3. Grill the shrimp for 2 minutes on each side or until it is thoroughly cooked and pink.

# Garlic Salmon Meal

TIME REQUIRED

22 minutes

SERVINGS

**3**

## INGREDIENTS

- Salmon fille  (2 @ 6 oz./ 170g each)
- Garlic (1 clove)
- Fresh rosemary (.25 tsp.)
- Salt (.25 tsp.)
- Lemon zest (1 tsp.)
- Pepper (.25 tsp.)

## DIRECTIONS

1. Mince the garlic and rosemary. Grate the lemon.
2. Measure and add all of the fixing except for the salmon into a mixing container.
3. Add the salmon to the mixture to marinate for 15 minutes.
4. Set the Foodi on the preheat setting using the medium setting for 6 minutes. Push the start button and wait for the beep. Add the salmon and set the unit to the grill function to cook for 3 minutes.
5. Turn the fis   and continue cooking for 3 more minutes to serve with your favorite side dishes.

# Grilled Citrusy Halibut

TIME REQUIRED

30 minutes

SERVINGS

**2**

## INGREDIENTS

- Orange & lime (1 each - zest and juice)
- Ginger (1 tsp.)
- Garlic (1 tsp.)
- Kosher salt (1 tsp.)
- Fresh parsley (1 tbsp.)
- Black pepper (1 tsp.)
- Canola oil (2 tbsp.)
- Honey (2 tbsp.)
- Frozen halibut fillet (2 @ 6 oz./ 170g each)

## DIRECTIONS

1. Insert the grill grate in the Ninja Foodi unit and close the hood.
2. Choose the grill mode at max temperature for 12 minutes. Hit the start button to begin preheating.
3. Meanwhile, prep the fixings Mince the garlic, ginger, and parsley. Zest and juice the orange and lime.
4. Thoroughly combine all of the fixing (except for the fillets in a mixing container. Add the fillet and cover them with the sauce.
5. When the unit beeps - it's preheated. Put the prepared fillet on the grill grate. Pour a spoonful of the marinade over the top of each one and close the hood. Cook until the internal temperature is 140°F/ 60° C (10-12 minutes).
6. For an additional infusion of flavor baste the fillet with marinade every 3 to 4 minutes.
7. At that time, they are ready to serve. Enjoy them with your favorite side dish.

# Pil Pil

TIME REQUIRED

20 minutes

SERVINGS

4

## INGREDIENTS

- Jumbo King prawns (20)
- Olive oil (3.5 fl oz./ 100 ml)
- Garlic (6-8 cloves)
- Lemon juice (half of 1 lemon)

**As Desired:**

- Chilli flake (1 large pinch)
- Sweet paprika powder
- Black pepper and salt

## DIRECTIONS

1. Clean and remove the heads from the prawns.
2. Insert the air fryer basket into the Ninja unit and close the hood. Select air fry at 360° F/180° C for 5 minutes. Push in the start button to begin preheating.
3. Once it beeps, add the prawns and cook for 4 to 5 minutes, turning once.
4. Add olive oil into a pan using the med-high temperature setting. When the oil is hot, mince and toss in the garlic and chili flakes
5. Cook for 2 to 3 minutes before adding in the prawns, a sprinkle of salt, sweet paprika powder, and pepper. Stir thoroughly and remove from the heat directly.
6. Give it a squirt of lemon juice and serve.

# Salmon Sliders

TIME REQUIRED

25 minutes

SERVINGS

8 sliders

## INGREDIENTS

- Lemon juice (half of 1 lemon)
- Onion (1 diced)
- Mustard (1 tbsp.)
- Fresh thyme (1 tbsp.)
- Mini burger buns
- Salmon (1 lb./ 450g)
- Breadcrumbs (.5 cup)

**To Garnish:**

- Lettuce
- Tomatoes
- Tartar sauce

## DIRECTIONS

1. Place the grill grate in the Ninja and close the hood.
2. Select the grill function for 9 minutes at MAX.
3. Push the start button to begin preheating the unit.
4. Chop the salmon in a food processor with other fixing except for the breadcrumbs.
5. Combine the salmon and breadcrumbs, shaping them into eight mini slider patties.
6. When the unit beeps, arrange the patties on the grill and shut the hood for 4 minutes.
7. About midway through the cycle, warm the buns on the grill or in the oven.
8. Garnish and serve the sliders as desired.

# Teriyaki Marinated Salmon

TIME REQUIRED
14 minutes +
marinate time (1-2 hours)

SERVINGS
4

## INGREDIENTS

- Uncooked skinless salmon fillet (4 @ 6 oz./ 170g each)
- Teriyaki marinade (1 cup)

## DIRECTIONS

1. Place fis fillet and teriyaki sauce in a large resealable plastic bag or container. Toss the fillet with the sauce. Refrigerate for at least 1 hour and up to 12 hours.
2. Insert the grill grate in The Foodi grill and close the hood.
3. Choose the grill mode and set the temperature to "max" for 8 minutes. Select the start function to begin preheating. When the unit beeps to signify it has preheated, put the fillet on the grill grate, gently pressing them down.
4. Close the hood and grill them for 6 minutes. There is no need to fli the fis during cooking.
5. Check the fillet for doneness (internal temperature should be 140° F/60° C. If necessary, close the top and continue cooking for up to 2 more minutes.
6. Serve fillet immediately.
7. Tip: Substitute your favorite marinade for the teriyaki sauce in step one.

# Swordfish With Caper Sauce

TIME REQUIRED

18 minutes

SERVINGS

**4**

## INGREDIENTS

- Drained capers (2 tbsp.)
- Olive oil (1 tbsp.)
- Pepper and salt (as desired)
- Lemon (1 into 8 wedges)
- Lemon juice (1 tbsp.)
- Unsalted butter (4 tbsp.)
- Swordfis steaks (4 @ 1 inch/ 2.5 cm thick)

## DIRECTIONS

1. Whisk the juice and oil in a mixing container.
2. Sprinkle the fis with pepper and salt on both sides and add it to the marinade to rest for 15 minutes.
3. Place the grill grate and close the hood. Select the start button to preheat the grill. Set it for 8 minutes on the max setting. When it beeps, add the fis and lock the hood to cook for 9 minutes.
4. Melt the butter in a saucepan and add the capers and lemon slices to simmer for 1 minute. Turn off the heat.
5. Transfer the fis to serving plates and serve with a portion of the sauce.

# CHAPTER 7

## Beef Favorites

# Bacon-Wrapped Tenderloin Filets

TIME REQUIRED

22 minutes

SERVINGS

4

## INGREDIENTS

- Uncooked bacon (8 strips)
- Beef tenderloin filet (4 center-cut @ 8 oz./ 225g each)
- Canola oil - divided (2 tbsp.)
- Ground black pepper & kosher salt (to your liking)
- Toothpicks (as needed)

## DIRECTIONS

1. Wrap two strips of bacon around the outside of each filet Securely close them using a toothpick.
2. Rub all sides of the wrapped filet with oil (using ½ tbsp. per filet) Dust them with salt and pepper.
3. Install the grill grate in the Ninja and close the hood. Choose the grill setting using the high-temperature setting (12 minutes). Hit the "start/stop" button to preheat.
4. Once it beeps, you are ready to arrange the filet on the grill grate. Gently press them down to ensure grill marks. Close the top and cook for 5 minutes.
5. Now, fli and close the hood and cook for 6 minutes (internal temperature should read 130° F/55° C on a food thermometer).
6. Transfer them to the countertop and wait about 10 minutes before serving. (They will continue to cook at a food-safe temperature.)
7. After that time, the juices should have redistributed evenly through the filets

# BBQ Beef Meatloaf

TIME REQUIRED

45-60 minutes

SERVINGS

**6-8**

## INGREDIENTS

- Ground beef/sirloin - ex. 90% lean ground sirloin (2 lb./ 900g)
- Eggs (2)
- Panko or plain breadcrumbs (1.5 cups)
- Lipton's onion soup (1 dry packet)
- Brown sugar bbq sauce - ex. Baby Rays (1 cup)
- Also Needed: 7 inch/ 18 cm Springform pan

## DIRECTIONS

1. In a mixing bowl, add the meat, panko or breadcrumbs, two eggs, and onion soup packet. Set the Ninja Grill on preheating. You can also set it to the "Max Grill" function to speed up the preheating phase.
2. Mix the meatloaf combination and add it to the springform pan, either with a parchment paper round on the bottom or a light non-stick spray to protect the pan when cutting into the meatloaf.
3. Add the meat mixture to the pan and brush on more BBQ sauce over the top. Place the pan on the rack - directly into the Ninja Foodi Grill.
4. Season the mini potatoes with a portion of red balsamic vinegar, oil, salt, and pepper. Set aside.
5. Set the grill to bake at 330° F/165° C. Set the timer for 40 minutes. After 15 minutes of cooking the meatloaf only, add the potatoes around the round pan.
6. Cover the top of the pan with tin foil.
7. Lightly brush the potatoes with more oil as desired.
8. When time is up, check the internal temperature of the meatloaf. It should be at 160° F/70° C. If so, and the potatoes are lightly browned, dinner is ready. Remove the inner tray from the grill and set it aside to cool. You can then place your pan on a serving plate and release the outer ring. Serve with a smile.

# The Classic Cheeseburgers

TIME REQUIRED

26 minutes

SERVINGS

4

## INGREDIENTS

- Uncooked ground beef (1.5 lb./ 700g @ 80% lean)
- Black pepper & Kosher salt (to your liking)
- American cheese (4 slices)
- Burger buns (4)

**Toppings Suggested:**

- Lettuce
- Tomatoes
- Red onion
- Pickles
- Condiments

## DIRECTIONS

1. Insert the grill grate in the unit and close the top. Set it on the grill function. Program the temperature setting to high for 8 minutes (medium-cooked burgers). Push the start button to preheat.
2. Meanwhile, divide the ground beef into four portions and shape them into loosely formed 4 inch/ 10 cm patties. Sprinkle them with pepper and salt. With your thumb, make a 1 inch/ 2.5 cm indent in the middle of each patty to help the burgers keep their shapes uniform during the cooking process.
3. When the unit beeps to signify it has preheated, arrange the patties on the grill grate. Close the hood and grill them for 6 minutes.
4. At that point, place a slice of cheese on each patty. Close the hood and continue cooking for another minute. Remove cheeseburgers from the grill grate.
5. Place the buns on the grill grate. Close the hood and grill them for the remaining 1 minute. When the cooking cycle is complete, serve cheeseburgers on the toasted buns.

# Frikadelle

TIME REQUIRED

30 minutes

SERVINGS

4

## INGREDIENTS

- Minced beef (14 oz./ 400g)
- Black pepper & salt (as desired)
- Garlic (2 cloves)
- Egg (1 large)
- Fresh breadcrumbs (4 tbsp.)
- Mustard (1 tbsp.)
- Ground cumin (.5 tsp.)
- Fresh parsley (1 tsp.)
- Fresh marjoram (.5 tsp.)
- For Coating: Dried breadcrumbs
- Optional: 1.7 fl. oz./ 50 ml cold water (if using - add extra 2 tbsp. of breadcrumbs)

## DIRECTIONS

1. Peel and mince the garlic. Finely chop the marjoram and parsley.
2. Suggested Tip: Add 1.7 fl. oz./ 50 ml of cold water to the minced beef before adding other ingredients. Let it chill in the fridge for an hour to make the burgers juicier after cooking.
3. Insert the grill plate in the unit and close the hood. Select the grill function, set the temperature setting to high for 10 minutes. Push the start button to begin preheating the Ninja unit.
4. Toss all of the fixing in a mixing container and prepare four patties. Lightly sprinkle them with breadcrumbs on both sides.
5. Once the grill has preheated, arrange the patties on the grill plate.
6. Close the hood and grill them for 5 minutes. Flip them over and continue cooking.
7. Serve hot with your favorite condiment with potatoes or on fresh toast.

# Grilled Steak Parmesan

TIME REQUIRED

15 minutes

SERVINGS

**2**

## INGREDIENTS

- Rump steaks (2)
- Tomato passata (7 oz./ 200g)
- Garlic clove (1 minced)
- Freshly chopped basil (1 tsp.)
- Dried oregano (.5 tsp.)
- Shredded mozzarella (1.15 oz./ 30g)
- Grated parmesan (.7 oz./ 20g)
- Salt and pepper (as desired)

## DIRECTIONS

1. Insert the Foodi grill plate into the unit and close the hood.
2. Choose the grill function set to high for 10 minutes. Push the "start/stop" button to begin preheating.
3. While the unit is preheating, combine the tomato passata with the garlic, basil, and oregano. Set to the side.
4. Generously season the steaks with salt and pepper.
5. After the Ninja beeps, it's preheated. Arrange the steaks on the grill plate. Close the hood to begin cooking.
6. When there are 5 minutes left on the timer, open the top and fli both steaks. Top each one with an equal amount of tomato sauce and a sprinkle of mozzarella and parmesan. Close the hood to continue cooking.
7. When ready, transfer the steaks from the cooker and set them to the side for about 5 minutes.
8. Serve garnished with basil and pasta to your liking.

# Pineapple Steak

TIME REQUIRED

18 minutes

SERVINGS

4

## INGREDIENTS

- Fillet mignon steaks (4 @ 6-8 oz./ 170-220g)
- Diced red onion (1 medium)
- Stemmed & diced jalapeno - seeded (1)
- Cored & diced pineapple (half of 1 medium)
- Canola oil (1 tbsp.)
- Lime juice (1 tbsp.)
- Chili powder (to taste)
- Chopped cilantro leaves (.25 cup)
- Pepper & salt (as desired)

## DIRECTIONS

1. Generously salt and pepper the fillet - rubbing it into the meat.
2. Set the Ninja grill for 8 minutes on high. After the beep, place the meat on the grill.
3. Grill it until it reaches 125° F/50° C (internal temp).
4. Combine the jalapeno with the pineapple and onion. Mix well.
5. Mix in the coriander, chili powder, and lime juice.
6. Serve the fillet with the pineapple topping.

# CHAPTER 8

## Intermediate Beef Favorites

# Cool Avocado Steak Salad

TIME REQUIRED

28 minutes

SERVINGS

4

## INGREDIENTS

- Ripe avocados(2)
- Cilantro leaves (1 cup)
- Salsa verde (2 cups)
- Beef flan  steak (2)
- Seeded tomatoes (2 medium)
- Salt and black pepper (.5 tsp. each)

## DIRECTIONS

1. Dice the avocado and steak. Remove the seeds from the tomatoes.
2. Season the steaks with pepper and salt.
3. Set the Foodi grill to preheat using the start button for 18 minutes using the medium temperature setting.
4. After you hear the beep, place the diced steak over the grill to cook for 9 minutes. Turn them over and continue cooking for another 9 minutes.
5. Meanwhile, add the salsa and cilantro to the blender until it's a fin mixture.
6. Serve the steak with the avocado, salsa, and tomatoes.

# London Broil

TIME REQUIRED

45 minutes + marinate time

SERVINGS

8

## INGREDIENTS

- London broil (1.5-2 lb./ 680-900g)

**The Marinade:**

- Soy sauce (.25 cup.)
- Garlic (3 tbsp.)
- Honey (2 tbsp.)
- Balsamic vinegar (.5 cup)
- Olive oil (2 tbsp.)
- Black pepper (2 tsp.)
- Onion powder (1 tsp.)
- Worcestershire sauce (1 tsp.)

## DIRECTIONS

1. Mince the garlic and measure the rest of the ingredients.
2. Mix all of the marinade fixings reserving a bit to use for dipping after the meat is cooked. Toss the meat into the marinade and give it as much time as possible to marinate in the fridge.
3. Insert the removable cooking pot and grill grate into the Ninja.
4. Choose the grill function set to high (500° F/260° C). Set the time for 10 minutes for a 1-1.5 inch/ 2.5-4 steak. The preheat cycle will take about 8 minutes.
5. Once "Add Food" flashes add the beef onto the grill, close the hood, and grill for 4 to 5 minutes. Turn the beef and close the lid. Grill for another 4 minutes and check the internal temperature to reach your personal preference.
6. Wait for about 5 minutes before cutting the meat to serve.

# New York Strip Steak & Asparagus

TIME REQUIRED

25 minutes

SERVINGS

**2-4**

## INGREDIENTS

- Uncooked New York strip steaks (2 @ 14-16 oz./ 400-450g each)
- Canola oil - divided (2 tbsp.)
- Ground black pepper and Kosher salt (to your liking)
- Asparagus - trimmed (1 bunch)

## DIRECTIONS

1. Brush each steak on all sides with ½ tablespoon canola oil, then sprinkle them with pepper and salt, as desired. Splash the asparagus with the rest of the oil. Dust them using pepper and salt also.
2. Insert the grill grate in the unit and close the hood. Select the grill function setting the temperature to "high" for 12 minutes. Select the start function to begin the preheating phase.
3. When you hear the beep, it has preheated. Add the steaks to the grill grate, gently pressing them down to maximize grill marks. Close the lid and set the timer for 4 minutes. At that time, turn the steaks over, close the hood, and cook for an additional 4 minutes (125° Fahrenheit or 50°Celsius for an internal temp).
4. Transfer the steaks to a holding container for about 5 minutes; they'll continue to cook to a food-safe temperature while resting. Use a cooking thermometer to ensure a food-safe temperature has been achieved.
5. In the meantime, arrange the asparagus on the grill grate. Close the hood and cook for 4 minutes. When cooking and resting are complete, slice the steak, and serve with the asparagus.

# Pot Roast

TIME REQUIRED
6 hours cook time & prep for 10 minutes

SERVINGS
6

## INGREDIENTS

**Seasoning Blend:**

- Garlic powder (1 tsp.)
- Black pepper (1 tsp.)
- Sea salt (2 tsp.)
- Dried thyme leaves (2 tsp.)
- Optional: Red pepper flake (.5 tsp.)
- Onion powder (1 tsp.)

**Roast Ingredients:**

- Avocado oil/another oil as desired (1-2 tbsp.)
- Chuck roast (3-4 lb./ 1.4-1.8kg)
- Vidalia onion (1)
- Beef stock - divided (4 cups)
- Optional: For gravy (.25 cup)
- Carrots (6)
- Gold potatoes (6 small)

## DIRECTIONS

1. Add the oil to the inner pan of the Foodi and preheat using the high-temperature setting (500°F/260°C).
2. Combine the seasoning in a mixing container. Rub onto both sides of the roast.
3. When the grill has preheated, arrange the roast on the bottom of the inner pan. Close the lid and grill on high for 5 minutes. Flip it over and grill it for another 5 minutes.
4. Cut the onion into chunks and add to the pan. Pour in two cups of beef stock and select the Roast function at 250°F/120°C (3 hours).
5. Flip the roast every hour if desired - not completely necessary. After the 3 hours, transfer the meat to a holding container.
6. Make the gravy by combining the rest of the beef stock and flou with some of the liquid in the pan into a large Mason jar or another glass container with a lid. Shake until thoroughly combined, and pour into the pan. Put the roast in along with the veggies. Set the grill to the roast setting at 250°F/ 120°C for another 3 hours.
7. Note: The total cook time will depend on your roast, so start checking it after the firs hour and fli it. It is ready when the meat is fork-tender, and the veggies are done as desired.

# Steak & Potatoes

TIME REQUIRED

1 hour

SERVINGS

4

## INGREDIENTS

- Russet potatoes (4)
- Steak (3 - 2 sirloins & 1 filet)
- Avocado oil (.25 cup)
- Steak seasoning (2 tbsp.)
- Sea salt (1 tbsp.)

## DIRECTIONS

1. Wash, dry, and poke holes in the potatoes with a fork.
2. Rub the oil over each one and sprinkle with salt. Arrange them in the air fryer basket.
3. Close the hood and set the unit to reach 400° F/ 200° C. Set the unit in the air fryer mode (35 minutes).
4. At that time, turn them over and continue cooking for another 10 minutes or until the center is fork-tender. Transfer them from the unit into a holding container and cover using a foil layer to keep warm.
5. Exchange the fryer basket for the grill piece inside the machine. Close the hood and set to grill at 500° F/260° C for 10 minutes.
6. Let it preheat while you sprinkle both sides of steak with seasoning, gently pressing the meat down into the mixture so it sticks.
7. Add the steaks. Cook the sirloin for 8 minutes, turning it halfway through. Cook the file  for 6 minutes turning after 4 minutes.
8. Wait for about 5 minutes after it reaches the desired doneness before slicing to serve.

# Steak & Vegetable Kebabs

TIME REQUIRED

27 minutes

SERVINGS

**4**

## INGREDIENTS

- New York strip steaks (2 @ 10–12 oz./ 280-340g each)
- White button mushrooms (8)
- Bell pepper - green/yellow/red (1)
- White onion - peeled & cut into quarters (1 small)
- Spices (as desired)
- Steak seasoning
- Black pepper
- Kosher salt

## DIRECTIONS

1. Insert the grill grate in the cooker and close the hood. Select the grill function using the high-temperature setting for 12 minutes. Choose start/stop to start preheating.
2. Meanwhile, slice the steaks, green peppers, and onions into 2 inch/ 5 cm cubes. Slice the mushrooms in half and remove the stems.
3. Assemble the skewers until they're almost full: Add the steak, mushroom, bell pepper, and onion. Be sure to push them nearly all of the way to the end of each skewer.
4. Liberally dust them using pepper, salt, and steak seasoning.
5. Once the unit beeps to signify it has preheated, arrange the prepared skewers on the grill grate. Close the hood and set the timer for 8 minutes without flipping.
6. Check each steak for the desired doneness, cooking up to 4 additional minutes if desired.
7. Serve and enjoy as a meal or quick party snack.

# CHAPTER 9

## Lamb - Pork & Other Favorites

# Indian Masala Lamb Chops

TIME REQUIRED

2 hours 30 minutes

SERVINGS

**8**

## INGREDIENTS

- Lamb chops (4.4 lb./ 70 oz./ 2kg)
- Natural yogurt (7 oz./ 200g)
- Oil (2.8 fl. oz./ 80 ml)
- Salt (1 tsp.)
- Kashmiri chili powder (1 tsp.)
- Paprika powder (.75 tsp.)
- Turmeric powder (.5 tsp.)
- Chilli flake (.5 tsp.)
- Garlic powder (1 tsp.)
- Ginger powder (.75 tsp.)
- Onion powder (1 tsp.)
- Coriander powder (1 tsp.)
- Cumin powder (1 tsp.)
- Garam masala powder (4 tsp.)
- Ground black pepper (.5 tsp.)

## DIRECTIONS

1. Marinate the chops in a large mixing container with all of the fixing listed for 2 hours.
2. Insert the grill plate in the unit. Choose the grill function and set the temperature to medium for 20 minutes. Push the start button to preheat.
3. Once ready, open and add four chops. Close the hood to start cooking. Flip after 5 minutes. Close the hood and check them at the 4-minute marker.
4. Cook for an additional minute if needed. Continue with the rest of the chops.
5. Serve with your favorite sides.

# Lamb Kebabs

TIME REQUIRED

47 minutes

SERVINGS

**8**

## INGREDIENTS

- Cumin seeds (2 tsp.)
- Minced lamb - not too lean (35 oz./ 1kg)
- Red onion - roughly chopped (1/4 of 1)
- Green chilies (3)
- Coriander (10 stalks)
- Garlic (5 cloves)
- Ginger crushed (1 inch/ 2.5 cm)
- Garam masala (1 tsp.)
- Red chili powder (1 tsp.)
- Salt (1.5 tsp.)
- Black pepper (1 tsp.)
- Optional: Cheddar cheese - grated (1.4 oz./ 40g)
- Wooden skewers (8 - soaked for a few hours)
- Oil for brushing (as needed)

## DIRECTIONS

1. Warm a dry skillet using the medium-temperature setting to dry-fry the cumin seeds for a minute. Watch them carefully. Transfer them from the pan and pour them into the bowl of a food processor, along with the rest of the fixings
   Process the mixture quickly to combine but don't over mix (this is just to bring the ingredients together). Alternatively, mix by hand.
2. Portion the mixture into eight balls. Squeeze onto the pre-soaked skewers. Put them in the fridge for 1/2 hour to make it easier to cook.
3. Insert the grill plate into the Ninja Foodi Grill and the air crisper unit. Close the hood.
4. Choose the grill function and set the temperature to the highest setting for 12 minutes. Brush the kebabs with oil and place them on the grill plate.
5. Close the hood and turn after 6 minutes. Check at 10 minutes to make sure they aren't browning too much. Serve when ready.

# Grilled Ribs

TIME REQUIRED

17 minutes

SERVINGS

6

## INGREDIENTS

- Boneless country-style pork ribs (2 lb./ 900g)
- BBQ sauce (.5 cup)
- Seasoning: Your choice

## DIRECTIONS

1. Preheat the grill using the high-temperature setting (12 minutes). Spray the grill grate with olive oil cooking spray.
2. Season the ribs to your liking and place them on the grill grates in the Foodi.
3. Coat with about ¼ cup of your favorite sauce.
4. Grill for 10 minutes. Carefully open the hood, turn the ribs, and add more sauce.
5. Continue grilling for 2 minutes until they reach 165° F or 75° C (internal temperature).
6. Serve them piping hot with your favorite side dish.

# Apple & Sage Pork Tenderloin

TIME REQUIRED

35 minutes

SERVINGS

4

## INGREDIENTS

- Pork tenderloin (1 whole)
- Apple (1 shredded)
- Bacon (3.5 oz./ 100g or about 8-10 rashers)
- Sage leaves (10 - finel chopped)
- Honey (1 tbsp.)
- Mustard (1 tbsp.)
- Butter (1 tbsp.)
- Salt and pepper (as desired)

## DIRECTIONS

1. Spread the tenderloin on a cutting board and cut a deep pocket through the whole length (0.8-1.2 inch/ 2-3 cm). Whisk the honey with the mustard and brush it over the meat - including the pocket.
2. Combine shredded apple with the butter, finel chopped sage, salt, and pepper. Load the stuffi into the meat pocket.
3. Use the Ninja Grill without the grill plate or crisper basket installed. Close the hood. Choose the roasting function set at 460° F/240° C for ½ hour. Start the preheating cycle by pressing the start button.
4. Meanwhile, wrap the tenderloin with bacon and secure the ends with a skewer.
5. When the unit beeps, arrange the tenderloin in the cooking pot. Close the top and cook it for ½ hour.
6. Open the hood every 10 minutes and brush the meat with the rest of the honey-mustard glaze.
7. When it's ready, carefully remove the tenderloin from the cooker and wait for 5 minutes before serving it hot with a side of mashed potatoes and veggies.

# Juicy Grilled Pork Chops

TIME REQUIRED

35-40 minutes

SERVINGS

**4**

## INGREDIENTS

- Pork chops (4 - bone-in or boneless)

**The Marinade:**

- Soy sauce (.75 cup)
- Brown sugar (.75 cup)
- Garlic (2 cloves)
- Onion (1)

## DIRECTIONS

1. Mince or chop the garlic and onion. Make the pork marinade and add them with the chops. Marinate them in the refrigerator before cooking (1/2 hour).
2. Insert removable cooking pot and grill grate into the Ninja.
3. Press the grill button, set to high (500° F/260° C) for 15 minutes.
4. Once the "Add Food" flashes arrange the chops on the grill and close the hood. Grill for 7 to 8 minutes, fli the meat, and close the lid. Cook for another 5 minutes. Check for doneness of an internal temperature of 150° F/70° C.
5. Wait for about 5 minutes before serving.

# Korean Pork Delight

TIME REQUIRED
18 minutes +
marinate time (6-8 hours)

SERVINGS
4

## INGREDIENTS

- Korean red chili paste (3 tbsp.)
- Sesame seeds (2 tbsp.)
- Red pepper flake
- Black pepper (3 tsp.)
- Soy sauce (.5 cup)
- Brown sugar (.5 cup)
- Yellow onion (1)
- Green onion (3 tbsp.)
- Garlic cloves (5)
- Pork (2 lb./ 900g)
- To Serve: Bed of lettuce

## DIRECTIONS

1. Slice the yellow onion and mince the cloves and green onion. Slice the pork into 0.15 inch/ 0.4 cm slices.
2. Toss each of the fixing into a zipper-type plastic baggie. Marinate it for 6 to 8 hours.
3. Warm the Ninja grill using the medium setting for 8 minutes.
4. When it beeps, it has preheated. Place the sliced pork over the grill and close the hood for 4 minutes.
5. Flip them over and continue to cook for another 4 minutes.
6. Serve over a layer of chopped lettuce.

# Chili Dogs

TIME REQUIRED

65 minutes

SERVINGS

**16**

## INGREDIENTS

**For the Chili:**

- Pasta/ tomato sauce jar (24 oz./ 680g - as desired)
- Butter (2 tsp.)
- Ground beef (2 lb./ 900g)
- Vegetable oil (2 tsp.)
- Chili powder (2 tsp./as desired)
- Minced garlic (4 cloves)
- White onion (1 finel chopped)
- Salt (2 tsp.)

**Also Needed:**

- Hot dog buns (16)
- Butter (2 tbsp.)
- Beef hot dogs (16)

## DIRECTIONS

1. Prepare the chili by warming the oil and butter to cook the burger with garlic and onions. Fry it for about 15 minutes.
2. Arrange the Ninja grill grate on the unit and close the lid. Select the grill setting for 10 minutes at Max.
3. Push the start/stop button to preheat the grill. When the unit buzzes, add the hotdogs and close the lid to the grill for 3 to 5 minutes. About midway, fli the dogs around.
4. Butter the buns and heat them on the grill or in the oven as desired.
5. Serve with chili and other desired toppings.

# Sausage & Pepper Grinders

TIME REQUIRED

41 minutes

SERVINGS

**6**

## INGREDIENTS

- Bell peppers (2)
- White onion (1)
- Canola oil - divided (2 tbsp.)
- Freshly cracked black pepper & kosher salt (as desired)
- Raw sausages - ex. hot Italian or Bratwurst (6 @ 4 oz./ 115g each)
- Hot dog buns (6)
- Condiments (as desired)

## DIRECTIONS

1. Insert the grill grate in the Foodi and close the hood. Choose the grill function, set the temperature to low for 26 minutes. Select the "start/stop" mode to begin preheating.
2. Meanwhile, cut the peppers into quarters, removing the ribs and seeds. Peel and slice the onion into 1 inch/ 2.5 cm rings.
3. Toss the peppers and onions with oil, black pepper, and salt.
4. After the Foodi has preheated, arrange the peppers and onions on the grill grate. Close the hood to grill them for 12 minutes without flipping
5. Transfer the onions and peppers into a mixing container and arrange the sausage on the grill grate. Securely close the hood and grill for 6 minutes.
6. Flip the sausage, close the lid, and continue cooking for 6 minutes.
7. Gently break apart the grilled onions into individual rings and mix them with the peppers.
8. When ready, remove the sausages from the grill grate.
9. Arrange the buns, cut-side down, on the grill grate, shut the hood, and grill for 2 minutes.
10. When they are ready, spread any desired condiments on the buns, and add the sausages. Top each liberally with peppers and onions to serve.

# CHAPTER 10

## Delicious Side Dish & Salad Favorites

# Air-Crisped Sweet Potato Wedges

TIME REQUIRED

34 minutes

SERVINGS

4

## INGREDIENTS

- Sweet potatoes or yams (2 @ approx. 1 lb./450g each)
- Canola oil (1 tbsp.)
- Honey (1 tbsp. + more for garnish)
- Ground black pepper (.5 tsp.)
- Smoked paprika (1 tsp. + more for garnish)
- Coarse-grind - kosher salt (1 tsp.)
- Dipping sauce of choice

## DIRECTIONS

1. Rinse and scrub the yams or potatoes thoroughly in cold water. Pat them until dry. Slice each potato in half lengthwise, then cut each half into 4 or 5 wedges.
2. Combine the rest of the fixing to coat the wedges.
3. Place the crisper basket in the unit and select the air crisp function. Set the temperature at 390° F/200° C for 24 minutes. Hit the start/stop button to begin preheating.
4. When the unit beeps to signify it has preheated, spread the wedges evenly in the basket, and close the hood to cook for 10 minutes.
5. Open the lid, toss or stir wedges with rubber-tipped tongs. Close the hood and continue cooking for another 10 minutes.
6. At that point, check wedges for doneness. If they need more time, cook for up to 4 more minutes until the wedges achieve the desired level of crispiness.
7. When ready, toss the wedges with honey and paprika, as desired, and serve with the dipping sauce of choice.

# Air-Fried Parmesan Brussel Sprouts

TIME REQUIRED

20 minutes

SERVINGS

**4**

## INGREDIENTS

- Fresh Brussel sprouts - cut in half lengthwise (17.5 oz./ 500g)
- Olive oil (1 tbsp.)
- Grated parmesan cheese (7 oz./ 200g)
- Pepper and salt (.25 tsp. each)

## DIRECTIONS

1. Insert the crisper basket into the unit and close the hood.
2. Choose the air fry function at 390° F/ 200° C. Push in the start button to begin preheating.
3. While the unit is preheating, slice the sprouts into halves and toss them into a large mixing container with salt, pepper, olive oil, and parmesan.
4. When the Ninja unit beeps to signify it has preheated, add the sprouts to the crisper basket. Close the top and set the timer for 10 minutes.
5. Use a pair of silicone coated tongs to toss the sprouts one to two times during the cooking cycle.
6. When it's ready, remove the sprouts from the crisper basket and serve promptly.

# Crispy Parmesan Potato Wedges

TIME REQUIRED
25 minutes

SERVINGS
4

## INGREDIENTS

- Potatoes (14 oz./400g)
- Oil (1 tbsp.)
- Grated parmesan (4 tbsp.)
- Flour (1 tbsp.)
- Rosemary (2 tsp.)
- Garlic (2 cloves)
- Pepper & salt (.5 tsp. each)

## DIRECTIONS

1. Finely chop the rosemary and mince the garlic.
2. Insert the crisper basket in the unit and close the hood. Choose the roast setting at 360° F/180° C for 10 minutes. Click the start button to begin the preheating cycle.
3. While the unit is preheating, slice the potatoes into 0.6 inch/ 1.5 cm thick wedges and toss with oil, salt, and pepper.
4. When the unit beeps, it's reheated, so add the potato wedges into the crisper basket and close the lid to begin cooking.
5. Sift or whisk the parmesan with the flour rosemary, and garlic. Set it to the side for now.
6. When cooking is complete, toss the potatoes in a container with the parmesan mixture and toss to evenly coat all of the potatoes.
7. Leaving the empty crisper basket in the unit, choose the air fry setting at 390° F/ 200° C for 10 minutes. When the unit beeps, open the hood and evenly spread potatoes in the crisper basket. Close the top to begin cooking.
8. Serve them promptly for flavorfu results.

# Green Beans Ninja-Style

TIME REQUIRED

15 minutes

SERVINGS

**4**

## INGREDIENTS

- Oil (2 tbsp.)
- Lemon juice (1 lemon)
- Freshly cracked black pepper & flak sea salt
- Trimmed green beans (1 lb./ 450g)

## DIRECTIONS

1. Trim the beans and place them into a bowl with the oil. Swirl them thoroughly.
2. Warm the Foodi grill to 'max' for 10 minutes.
3. When the preheat cycle is completed, it will beep. Place the beans on the grill and cook for 10 minutes. Toss them about midway through the cycle.
4. Serve with a squeeze of juice, salt, and black pepper.

# French Fries With Parmesan & Garlicky Mayo

TIME REQUIRED

40-45 minutes

SERVINGS

**5-6**

## INGREDIENTS

- Frozen french fries (1 lb./ 450g)
- Mayonnaise (.5 cup)
- Garlic - minced (2 cloves)
- Garlic powder (1 tsp.)
- Ground black pepper (.25 tsp.)
- Kosher salt (.5 tsp.)
- Lemon juice (1 squeeze)
- Canola oil (1 tbsp.)
- Parmesan cheese (.5 cup)
- Parsley (1 tbsp.)

## DIRECTIONS

1. Insert the crisper basket unit and close the hood.
2. Choose the air crisp mode at 375°F/190°C for 22 minutes. Push the start button to begin preheating.
3. When the unit beeps - it's preheated. Toss the frozen fries into the basket and close the lid to cook for 10 minutes.
4. At that time, shake the basket of fries, and close the hood to resume cooking.
5. Meanwhile, whisk the mayo with the garlic, garlic powder, salt, pepper, and lemon juice in a mixing container. Set aside until time to serve.
6. After 10 minutes, check the fries for doneness. Continue cooking up to 2 additional minutes if necessary.
7. Chop the parsley and grate the parmesan.
8. When ready, toss the fries with canola oil, parmesan, and parsley. Serve immediately with the garlicky mayo sauce.

# Grilled Broccoli

TIME REQUIRED

23 minutes

SERVINGS

**6**

## INGREDIENTS

- Broccoli (1 head)
- Garlic (2 tbsp.)
- Honey (1 tbsp.)
- Olive oil (1 tbsp.)
- Soy sauce (3 tbsp.)
- Balsamic vinegar (3 tbsp.)
- Optional: Parmesan (.25 cup)

## DIRECTIONS

1. Insert the removable cooking pot and the grill grate into the Foodi.
2. Press the grill button, set the temperature to “max for 10 minutes. Press the start function for preheating.
3. Chop the broccoli into floret and mince the garlic.
4. Measure and add the vinegar, soy sauce, honey, garlic, and oil into a zipper-type bag. Toss them gently to combine.
5. Add the broccoli and shake it again to marinate it for about 10 minutes.
6. Once "Add Food" flashes add the marinated broccoli on top of the grill grate.
7. Cook for 10 minutes, turning the floret every few minutes to ensure even cooking.
8. Transfer the broccoli from the grate to a platter and sprinkle with parmesan cheese to serve.
9. Cooking Tip: If you do not have a grill basket, be sure to cut larger floret so they don't fall between the grates. Grill on top of the grates, frequently tossing them.

# Honey & Herb Charred Carrots

TIME REQUIRED

40-45 minutes

SERVINGS

**4-6**

## INGREDIENTS

- Honey (1 tbsp.)
- Kosher salt (1 tsp.)
- Melted butter (2 tbsp.)
- Medium carrots (6)
- Fresh parsley & rosemary (1 tbsp. of each)

## DIRECTIONS

1. Insert the grill grate in the Foodi and close the hood.
2. Set it to the grill function with the temperature to "max" for 10 minutes. Select the start function to begin preheating.
3. Chop the rosemary and parsley, and set it aside.
4. Whisk the honey with the salt and melted butter.
5. Peel and slice the carrots - lengthwise. Coat them with the honey butter, then rub evenly with the fresh herbs.
6. When the unit beeps, it's ready to arrange the carrots in the center of the grill grate. Close the hood and cook for 5 minutes.
7. At that point, shake/turn the carrots. Close the lid and cook for the remaining 5 minutes.
8. When cooking is complete, serve and enjoy it right away for the best flavor results.

# Grilled Goat Cheese Crostini With Figs

TIME REQUIRED

9 minutes

SERVINGS

2

## INGREDIENTS

- Goat's cheese (8 slices)
- Figs (2 sliced)
- Ciabatta bread (4 slices)
- Rocket/arugula leaves (1 handful)
- Spinach (1 handful - shredded)
- Balsamic vinegar (2 tbsp.)
- Lavender honey (2 tbsp.)
- Mustard (1 tbsp.)
- Oil (2 tbsp.)
- Black pepper & salt (as desired)
- Optional: Poached fruit - ex. - pears

## DIRECTIONS

1. Insert the pot and grill plate in the Ninja unit and close the hood.
2. Choose the grill function at 500° F/ 260° C for 4 minutes. Push the start button to begin preheating.
3. Lay the sliced bread down firs and add a layer of goat's cheese and fi slices to it.
4. Whisk the honey with the balsamic vinegar, mustard, oil, salt, and pepper. Thoroughly combine to make the dressing.
5. Once the grill is preheated, place the bread with fig and cheese on the grill plate and close the hood to begin the cooking process.
6. Place the arugula and spinach on a plate to prepare for serving.
7. When ready, remove bread from the Foodi unit and place it on top of the rocket and spinach.
8. Dress with honey balsamic dressing and serve promptly for the best flavo results.

# Italian Spiced Squash

TIME REQUIRED

26 minutes

SERVINGS

**4**

## INGREDIENTS

- Olive oil (1 tbsp.)
- Dried oregano (1.5 tsp.)
- Black pepper (.25 tsp.)
- Salt (.5 tsp.)
- Dried thyme (1 tsp.)
- Butternut squash (1 medium)

## DIRECTIONS

1. Peel the squash and slice it into ½ inch/ 1.3 cm slices.
2. Combine all of the fixing and add the sliced squash.
3. Set the Ninja grill for 16 minutes using the medium setting. Start the timer to preheat by clicking the start button.
4. When the unit beeps, add the squash to the grill and close the hood to cook for 8 minutes.
5. Open the lid and fli the squash. Close the hood and finis cooking.
6. Serve when ready as desired.

# Loaded Baked Potato

TIME REQUIRED

65 minutes

SERVINGS

**4-5**

## INGREDIENTS

- Russet potatoes (5 @ 6–8 oz./ 170-225g each)
- Unsalted butter - divided (5 tsp.)
- Shredded cheddar cheese - divided (1.66 oz./ 50g or 1-2/3 cups)
- Sour cream (1.25 cups)
- Cooked bacon - chopped (7 slices)
- Fresh scallions - chopped (1 bunch)

## DIRECTIONS

1. Remove the crisper basket and grill grate from the cooker. Choose the Bake function at 390° F/200° C.
2. Set the timer at 40 minutes. Choose the start/pause function to warm the grill.
3. Pierce the potatoes three times. When the unit beeps to signify it has preheated, arrange the potatoes in the cooker and close the lid. Set again the timer at 40 minutes.
4. Transfer them to the countertop to cool for about 5 minutes.
5. At that time, make a 3 inch/ 7.5 cm cut lengthwise in each potato.
6. Press each end of the potatoes toward one another to make an opening, and add one teaspoon butter of butter with 1/3 cup cheese to each potato.
7. Close the hood and choose the bake function at 375° F/190° C. Set the timer for 8 minutes. Select "start/stop" to preheat.
8. When it beeps, arrange the potatoes in the cooker and cook them for 8 minutes.
9. Lastly, remove potatoes and top each with ¼ cup sour cream and one tablespoon chopped bacon. Garnish with scallions and serve promptly.

# Mexican Street Corn

TIME REQUIRED

30 minutes

SERVINGS

4

## INGREDIENTS

- Corn (4 eats)
- Canola oil - divided (2 tbsp.)
- Ground black pepper & kosher salt (to taste)

**The Sauce:**

- Cotija cheese, grated (1 cup + more for the garnish)
- Sour cream (.25 cup)
- Mayonnaise (.25 cup)
- Lime juice (2 limes)
- Onion powder (1 tsp.)
- Freshly chopped cilantro (.25 cup)
- Garlic powder (1 tsp.)

## DIRECTIONS

1. Insert grill grate in the Ninja unit and close the hood.
2. Choose the grill mode with the temperature set to max for 12 minutes. Begin preheating by pushing the start button.
3. Meanwhile, shuck the corn and brush them using ½ tablespoon of oil. Season it to your liking with pepper and salt.
4. When the unit beeps, it's time to place the corn on the grill grate. Close the top and grill them for 6 minutes.
5. At that time, fli the corn. Close the hood and continue cooking for the remaining 6 minutes.
6. Meanwhile, combine the sauce.
7. When cooking is complete, coat the corn with sauce. Garnish with additional cotija cheese and serve right away.
8. Note: For an easy-to-eat salad, cut the grilled corn off the cob and mix with half the mayo mixture.

# Rice & Vegetable Stuffed Peppers

TIME REQUIRED

47 minutes

SERVINGS

6

## INGREDIENTS

- Red/green bell peppers (6)
- Garlic (4 cloves)
- White onion - peeled (1 small)
- Instant rice - cooked (2 bags @ 8.5 oz./ 240g each)
- Red enchilada sauce (10 oz./ 280g can)
- Fajita spice mix (1 oz./ 30g pkg.)
- Diced green chilis (4 oz./ 115g can about 2/3 cup)
- Vegetable stock (.5 cup)
- Shredded Colby Jack cheese - divided (8 oz./ 225g bag)

## DIRECTIONS

1. Mince the garlic and onions. Cook the rice. Drain the chilis.
2. Prep the peppers by topping ½ inch/ 1.3 cm sections and reserving them. Remove the seeds and ribs from the insides. Chop the ½ inch/ 1.3 cm portions of reserved bell peppers and place them in a big mixing container. Mix in all other fixings except whole bell peppers and half of the cheese.
3. Use the Ninja cooking pot without a grill grate or crisper basket installed.
4. Close the hood. Choose the roast mode at 350° F/ 180° C. Set the timer to 32 minutes. Push the "start/stop" to trigger preheating.
5. In the meantime, spoon the mixture into the peppers, fillin them to the top.
6. Once preheated, arrange the peppers, standing upright, in the unit. Close the hood and cook for 30 minutes.
7. Sprinkle the rest of the cheese over the peppers. Close the lid and continue cooking for 2 minutes.
8. When cooking is complete, serve promptly.

# Samosas

TIME REQUIRED

1 hour 25 minutes

SERVINGS

**25**

## INGREDIENTS

- Ghee/oil (3 tbsp.)
- Onion (3 diced)
- Ginger paste (1 tbsp.)
- Cloves of garlic (6-7 - crushed)
- Green chilies (2-3 -crushed)
- Salt (as desired)
- Coriander powder (1 tbsp.)
- Cumin powder (1 tbsp.)
- Chopped coriander (1 handful)
- Cumin seeds (1 tbsp.)
- Chicken mince - white meat (35 oz./ 1kg)
- Samosa pastry sheets (20-25)
- Flour (1 tbsp.)
- Water (3 tbsp.)

## DIRECTIONS

1. Prepare a skillet using the medium-temperature setting. Heat the oil. Dice and add the onions, garlic, ginger, and green chili. Sauté them for 5 minutes until they are lightly golden.
2. Mix in all the spices and salt. Continue to sauté for a minute before stirring in the mince. Cover and cook using the low setting for 45 minutes, or until the meat is cooked and dried out.
3. Uncover and if there is any water remaining, keep the mixture on the heat until it dries out as much as possible. Add in the chopped coriander and leave it to cool.
4. Prepare a paste from the flour and water and set aside.
5. Carefully strip out one sheet from the pastry bundle and lay it straight.
   Cover the remaining pastry with a damp muslin cloth.
6. Place a small portion of the samosa mixture onto the left corner. Fold into a triangle and continue to turn until there is a thin rectangular bit of pastry left hanging. Seal the samosa by adding a little paste to the remaining edge, then fold and press in gently.
7. Repeat the process for the remainder of the samosas.
8. Preheat the grill using the air fryer function for 5 minutes using the high setting. Brush the samosas with oil.
9. Arrange seven or eight samosas in the basket and cook until golden brown turning in between (15-18 minutes).
10. Repeat the process for the remaining Samosas and serve.

# Roasted Red Potatoes

TIME REQUIRED

23 minutes

SERVINGS

**4**

## INGREDIENTS

- Red/yellow potatoes (3 lb./ 1.4kg/ 6 large)
- Avocado oil
- Italian seasoning (coating)
- Pepper & salt (as desired)
- Yellow onion (1)

## DIRECTIONS

1. Rinse the potatoes and pat dry. Quarter the potatoes. Slice your onions on the thicker side and add them to a large mixing container. Drizzle them using avocado oil and mix to be sure all potatoes are coated. Don't use olive oil.
2. Sprinkle them with salt, pepper, and Italian seasoning to coat lightly.
3. Lightly prep the inner basket of the grill with avocado oil. Add potatoes to the basket. Push the start button to grill 375° F/190° C using the roast option for 20 to 23 minutes. Midway through, check the potatoes and lightly toss them to be sure all are roasting evenly. Spritz with more avocado oil if needed. You may add more time for the desired crispness. Garnish with rosemary sprigs to serve.

# Stuffed Mushrooms

TIME REQUIRED

13 minutes

SERVINGS

4

## INGREDIENTS

- Champignon mushroom caps (4 large - washed)
- Breadcrumbs (1.8oz./ 50g)
- Fresh parsley (finel chopped) (1 tbsp.)
- Cream cheese (6 oz./ 170g)
- Fresh garlic (1 clove)
- Walnuts (1.4 oz./ 40g)
- Nutmeg (1/8 tsp.)
- ½ tsp cayenne pepper (.5 tsp.)
- Salt and pepper (as desired)
- For Brushing: olive oil

## DIRECTIONS

1. Finely chop the parsley, walnuts, and mince the garlic.
2. Divide mixture into 4 equal parts and create balls.
3. Insert the grill plate into the Ninja Foodi Grill & Air Fryer and close the lid. Select the grill function with the temperature to "med" for 8 minutes. Push the start button to begin preheating.
4. Meanwhile, lightly brush the mushroom caps with olive oil and a sprinkle of salt and pepper. Place individual stuffi balls on top of the mushroom caps and press gently.
5. Once the unit beeps, place the stuffe mushrooms on the grill plate. Close the hood and cook for 8 minutes. When the cooking cycle is complete, serve the mushrooms promptly for the best results.

# Tandoori Cauliflower

TIME REQUIRED

20 minutes

SERVINGS

4

## INGREDIENTS

- Cauliflowe  (1 medium)

**The Marinade:**

- Greek yogurt (.5 cup)
- Garlic (4 cloves)
- Ginger (2 inch/ 5 cm chunk)
- Red chili powder (.5 tsp.)
- Garam masala (1 tsp.)
- Turmeric powder (.5 tsp.)
- Gram flou  (1 tbsp.)
- Curry powder - ex. - madras (1 tsp.)
- Optional: Dried fenugreek (1 tsp.)
- Oil for brushing

## DIRECTIONS

1. Chop the cauliflowe  into florets Mince the garlic and ginger. Mix each of the marinade fixing  in a large mixing container. Add the cauliflowe  floret  and stir.
2. Attach the air crisper basket to the Ninja Foodi Health Grill & Air Fryer AG301.
3. Put the floret  into the air fryer basket and brush with oil.
4. Set to 360° F/180° C and bake for 16 to 18 minutes. Check about halfway through the cooking cycle, and brush with more oil if necessary.

# CHAPTER 11

## Easy Appetizers & Snacks

# Air-Crisped Pickle Spears With Special Sauce

TIME REQUIRED

33 minutes

SERVINGS

**4**

## INGREDIENTS

- Dill pickle (12 spears)
- All-purpose flou (1 cup)
- Eggs (2 whole & 1 white)
- Seasoned coating mix (4.5 oz./ 130g box)
- Cooking oil spray (as needed)
- Yellow mustard (2 tbsp.)
- Mayo (2 tbsp.)
- Ketchup (2 tbsp.)

## DIRECTIONS

1. Gather three mixing containers. Add flou to a shallow bowl. Whisk all of the eggs for one minute in another shallow container. In a third shallow bowl, add the seasoned coating mix.
2. Pat the pickle spears dry. Toss two pickles in flou until evenly coated. Gently tap off any excess flour then coat in the egg wash. Transfer them to the breadcrumbs, tossing well to evenly coat. Put the pickles on a platter and continue with the rest of the pickles. Pop the platter of pickles in the freezer to set for ½ hour.
3. Insert the crisper basket in the unit and close the hood. Select the unit to air crisp for 18 minutes at 375° F/190° C. Begin the preheat cycle using the "start/stop button. Transfer the pickles from the freezer and spray all sides with cooking spray.
4. When the unit beeps, it's preheated. Place the pickles evenly in the basket and close the hood to cook for 9 minutes.
5. Meanwhile, whisk the mayo, ketchup, and mustard in a mixing container to make the sauce and set aside.
6. Flip the pickles using rubber-tipped tongs and resume cooking for 7 minutes.
7. Check the pickles for doneness. You can cook for another 2 minutes as needed.
8. When they're ready, carefully transfer the pickles using rubber-tipped tongs and serve to enjoy promptly with sauce.

# Air-Fried Jalapeno Poppers

TIME REQUIRED

50 minutes

SERVINGS

4

## INGREDIENTS

- Cashews (5.8 oz./170g)
- Water (2.8 fl. oz./80ml)
- Juice of 1 lemon
- Coconut oil (1 tsp.)
- Nutritional yeast (1 tbsp.)
- Himalayan pink salt (.5 tsp.)
- Garlic powder (.5 tsp.)
- Fresh coriander (1 handful - chopped)
- Black pepper (.25 tsp.)
- Optional: Fresh chives - chopped (1 tbsp.)
- Fresh dill (1 tsp. - chopped)
- Jalapenos or large mild green chilies (16)

**The Breadcrumbs:**

- Almond flou (3.5 oz./ 100g/ .875 cup)
- Arrowroot flour cornstarch (3.5 oz./ 100g)
- Smoked paprika (.75 tsp.)
- Sea salt (1 pinch)
- Garlic powder (.75 tsp.)
- Plant-based milk (6.5 fl. oz./ 185 ml)
- Cooking spray (as needed)

## DIRECTIONS

1. Soak the cashews overnight.
2. Combine all of the ingredients for the stuffe chilies (omit the fresh herbs, jalapeños, and breadcrumb ingredients) into a food processor. Blend until it's smooth. Pulse in the freshly chopped herbs, transfer the mixture to a bowl and cover with a cling plastic film and chill.
3. Take each whole chili and, using a small sharp knife, make an incision along the length. Only cut one side and not the entire way through. Open up the cavity carefully and, using the opposite end of a teaspoon, scrape out and discard the seeds. If you like a little heat, leave some seeds in! If you aren't a spice fan, be sure to remove the membrane too.
4. Transfer the fillin for the poppers into a piping bag and carefully pipe the mixture into the cavity of each chili until almost full.
5. Whisk the almond flou with the arrowroot flour spices, and salt into a shallow bowl.
6. Place the milk into a separate bowl.
7. Dip each stuffe chili into the milk, and roll it in the breadcrumb mixture. Repeat if necessary, then place onto a plate. Repeat until all of the chilies have been breaded.
8. Insert the crisper basket into the Ninja unit. Choose the air fry function with the temperature set to 360° F/180° C for 10 minutes. Close the hood and let the machine run its pre-heat cycle.
9. When it buzzes, add half of the chilies to the crisper basket and let the program run. You can turn halfway through the cycle. Remove the chilies from the basket and cook the 2nd batch in the same manner. Serve immediately with your favorite condiments.
10. Notes: If you have any fillin leftovers, mix them with a little water and a splash of apple cider vinegar to use as a dip!

# Baked Apple Chips

TIME REQUIRED

1 hour 10 minutes

SERVINGS

**1**

## INGREDIENTS

- Cinnamon (1 tsp.)
- Honey (1 tsp.)
- Apples (2)

## DIRECTIONS

1. Set the Ninji on the bake cycle at 390° F/200° C. Set the preheat cycle by pushing the start button.
2. Slice the apples and combine them with the rest of the fixings Place them on the grill rack.
3. Cook for 45 minutes, checking and turning them at the halfway marker. Continue cooking until they have dried somewhat or to your liking.

# Air-Fried Tomato Slices

TIME REQUIRED

25 minutes

SERVINGS

**2**

## INGREDIENTS

- Egg (1 medium)
- Flour (.5 cup)
- Salt (.5 tsp.)
- Minced garlic (1 squashed)
- Grated cheddar cheese (1 tbsp.)
- Milk (1/8 cup)
- Cilantro & rosemary (.25 tbsp. each)
- Pepper (1/3 tsp.)
- Breadcrumbs (.25 cup)
- Firm tomatoes - sliced (2)

## DIRECTIONS

1. Attach the Foodi crisper basket into the Ninja unit and close the hood.
2. Select the air fry function and push the start button to begin preheating the unit.
3. Whisk the eggs in with the milk. In another dish, whisk the flou with salt and pepper. In the last one, mix the herbs, garlic, and breadcrumbs.
4. Dip each slice in a dish - beginning with the eggs.
5. Lightly spritz with oil and place a few slices at a time into the crisper basket. Cook for 2 to 3 minutes until nicely browned, shaking it occasionally for even frying.
6. Cool slightly before serving.

# BBQ Chicken Egg Rolls

TIME REQUIRED

17 minutes

SERVINGS

**6**

## INGREDIENTS

- Vegetable oil (to air fry)
- Diced onion (1)
- Barbecue sauce (1 cup)
- Freshly chopped spinach (.5 cup)
- Chopped bell pepper (1)
- Prepackaged egg roll wrappers
- Cubed cooked chicken (2 cups)
- Sweet corn (1 cup)
- Shredded cheese (2 cups)
- Black pepper (.25 tsp.)
- Salt (.5 tsp.)

## DIRECTIONS

1. Combine the bbq sauce with the chicken and pop it into the fridge to marinate for 1 hour.
2. Attach the crisper basket to the Ninja unit and close the hood. Select the air fry function and push the start button to begin the preheating cycle.
3. Toss the veggies with the herbs and chicken in a mixing container. Toss in the rest of the fixings thoroughly tossing.
4. Spoon about two tablespoons of the mixture into the middle of each wrapper. Lightly spritz them with cooking oil.
5. Arrange them in small batches in the Ninja unit for one to 2 minutes until they're nicely browned. Be sure to shake the basket occasionally for even crisping. Enjoy them with your preferred dip.

# Beef Liver Pate

TIME REQUIRED
35 minutes +
8 hours chilling time

SERVINGS
4

## INGREDIENTS

- Beef liver (21 oz./ 600g)
- Shallots (2)
- Butter - melted (4.2 oz./ 120g)
- Garlic clove (1)
- Bay leaves (2)
- Fresh thyme (.5 tbsp.)
- Brandy (3.5 fl oz./ 100 ml)
- Double/heavy cream (4 tbsp.)
- Black pepper and salt (as desired)

## DIRECTIONS

1. Clean and thinly slice the liver. Peel and dice the garlic clove and shallots. Finely chop the thyme.
2. Use the Ninja cooking pot without a grill plate or crisper basket installed.
3. Close the hood and choose the roast setting at 390° F/200° C for 20 minutes. Push the "start/stop" button to begin preheating.
4. When the Foodi unit beeps to signify it has preheated, add all of the fixing except for the cream. Close the hood and roast for 20 minutes.
5. When completed, remove the cooking pot and let the fixing cool down for 15 minutes.
6. Discard the bay leaves and pour the rest of the mixture into a blender with cream.
7. Blend until smooth for 5 minutes.
8. Once smooth, divide the pate into four individual ramekins and chill them in the fridge for 8 hours.
9. Enjoy the spread over thinly sliced toasts or as part of a charcuterie board!

# Cheesy Dumplings

TIME REQUIRED

25 minutes

SERVINGS

**8**

## INGREDIENTS

- Wonton wraps
- For coating: Vegetable oil
- Salt (.5 tsp.)
- Grated cheddar cheese (1 bag)
- Chopped green onions (2)
- Garlic powder (1 tsp.)

## DIRECTIONS

1. Secure the crisper basket in the Ninja unit and set the air fryer function. Preheat by choosing the start button.
2. Microwave the cheese to melt it and mix in the remainder of the fixings
3. Stuff the wrappers with the mixture and arrange them in the crisper basket. Cook them until golden (2-3 minutes).
4. Shake the basket for even crisping and serve promptly.

# Chili & Cheddar Cheese Zucchini Fries

TIME REQUIRED

17 minutes

SERVINGS

**2**

## INGREDIENTS

- Air frying oil (as needed)
- Flour (.5 cup)
- Pepper & salt (as desired)
- Chili powder (.5 tbsp.)
- Grated cheddar cheese (1 cup)
- Medium zucchini (1 - sliced to fry size)
- Breadcrumbs (.5 cup)
- Egg (1 large)

## DIRECTIONS

1. Add the Foodi crisper basket in the Ninja unit and shut the hood. Select the air fry function and push the start button to begin preheating.
2. Sprinkle the 'fries' with pepper and salt.
3. Whisk the eggs in a dipping dish.
4. In another container, mix the breadcrumbs with the cheese and seasoning.
5. Add one other container for flour
6. After the zucchini is sliced into fries, dip then in the bowls, starting with the egg. Lightly cover them with oil and place them in the crisper basket to cook.
7. Be sure to shake the basket for even crisping. Serve with your favorite dip.

# Courgette Chips

TIME REQUIRED

30 minutes

SERVINGS

**4**

## INGREDIENTS

- Courgette (1)
- Oil (1 tbsp.)
- Salt and pepper (as desired)
- Smoked paprika (.5 tsp.)
- Garlic powder (.5 tsp.)

## DIRECTIONS

1. Cut the courgette into 0.1 inch/ 2 mm slices.
2. Insert the crisper basket in Ninja and close the hood. Choose the air fry setting, set the temperature to 340° F/ 170° C, and set a timer for 20 minutes. Choose “start/stop” to preheat.
3. Slice the courgette and spread the slices on a paper towel to absorb as much liquid as possible.
4. Combine each of the fixing into a mixing container. Toss until the courgette is thoroughly covered.
5. When the Ninja beeps to signify it has preheated, arrange the seasoned courgette slices in the crisper basket. Spread them out and close the hood to begin the cooking process.
6. When the time has elapsed, remove the crisper basket from the Foodi unit and let them cool.
7. Serve cold and keep the chips in a closed container for a delicious treat for up to seven days.

# Crispy Breaded Asparagus With Creamy Pesto Dip

TIME REQUIRED

20 minutes

SERVINGS

**2**

## INGREDIENTS

- Green asparagus with woody ends chopped off (7-9 oz./ 200-250g)
- Grated parmesan (2.1 oz./60g)
- Ground or finel chopped almonds (1.7 oz./50g)
- Egg (1)
- Salt & pepper (1 dash of each)

**The Dip:**

- Sour cream (5.3 oz./150g)
- Pesto (1 tbsp.)
- Black pepper and salt (as desired)

## DIRECTIONS

1. Mix the parmesan and the almonds in a shallow container.
   Whisk the egg with the salt and pepper in a second shallow dish.
2. Coat the asparagus spears by dredging them firs in the egg mixture, then in the parmesan-almond mixture. (For a thick breading, dredge the spears twice).
3. Arrange the coated spears on a large sheet of parchment baking paper.
4. Insert the crisper basket in Ninja Grill and close the hood. Choose the air fry mode and set the temperature to 340° F/170° C.
5. Push the "start" button to begin preheating.
6. When the Ninja unit beeps, gently put the asparagus spears into the crisper basket in a single layer. Close the hood and set the timer for 10 minutes.
7. Prepare the dip by combining the sour cream with the pesto, salt, and pepper in a small mixing container.
8. When cooking is complete, check the spears for readiness – they should be golden brown and crispy. For thicker spears, add an additional 2 to 5 minutes of cooking time may be needed.
9. Carefully remove the asparagus with tongs and serve immediately with the dip.

# Crispy Cheddar Onions

TIME REQUIRED

35 minutes

SERVINGS

**12**

## INGREDIENTS

- Breadcrumbs (4 cups)
- Large onions (4)
- Medium eggs (4)
- Flour (2.5 cups)
- Grated cheddar cheese (2 cups)
- Baking powder (2 tsp.)
- To Coat: Vegetable oil (as needed)

## DIRECTIONS

1. Put the Foodi crisper basket on the Ninja unit and close the hood. Select the air-fry mode and push the start button to begin preheating.
2. Slice the onions into rings. Put the flou  and baking powder in one dish. In another container, whisk the eggs, and the last one - add the seasoning with the breadcrumbs.
3. Dip the slices in each of the dishes - starting with the eggs.
4. Place them in the crisper and air fry for 2 to 3 minutes until nicely browned, gently shaking if needed.
5. Serve them with your favorite dipping sauce.

# Curry Chicken Skewers With Mint Dip

TIME REQUIRED

1 hour 20 minutes

SERVINGS

4

## INGREDIENTS

- Chicken breasts (4)
- Tomato puree (1 tbsp.)
- Rapeseed oil (1 tbsp.)
- Garlic powder (1 tsp.)
- Turmeric (.25 tsp.)
- Garam masala (.25 tsp.)
- Ginger powder (.25 tsp.)
- Chili powder (1 tsp.)
- Plain yogurt (5.3 oz./ 150g)
- Salt and pepper (as desired)
- Cucumber – grated (half of 1)
- Mint leaves (10)

**To Garnish:**

- Coriander leaves (optional)
- Lemon juice (1 tbsp.)

## DIRECTIONS

1. Chop the chicken into 1.5 inch/ 4 cm cubes
2. Combine chicken with tomato puree, oil, and all spices in a large mixing container. Set it to the side and marinate for 1 hour.
3. Grate and combine the cucumber with the finel chopped mint, yogurt, lemon juice, salt, and pepper. Pop it into the fridge until serving time.
4. Insert the grill plate in the Foodi unit and close the hood. Choose the grill setting set at max for 10 minutes. Preheat it using the start button.
5. While it is getting ready, assemble the skewers until they're almost full.
6. Once the grill is preheated, add the skewers to the grill plate. Shut the hood and cook for 5 minutes.
7. Flip the skewers and continue cooking to the end of the cycle. Serve them piping hot with mint dip.

# Pigs In a Blanket

TIME REQUIRED
25 minutes

SERVINGS
6

## INGREDIENTS

- White cheese (1 slice)
- Onion powder (.25 tsp.)
- Hot dogs (2)
- Salted butter (1 tbsp.)
- Mustard (1 tbsp.)
- Garlic (.5 of 1 clove)
- Pastry premade rolled triangles

## DIRECTIONS

1. Set the Foodi at 350° F/180° C using the bake function. Push the start button to preheat.
2. Slice the hot dog into thirds and arrange them onto a triangle with a piece of cheese.
3. Brush the dough strips with a little mustard and bake until browned (around 12 minutes).
4. Crush the garlic. Meanwhile, melt the butter and mix in the garlic. Brush the pastry with the mixture when it's ready to serve.

# Mozzarella Sticks

TIME REQUIRED
17 minutes
+ 1 hour freezing time

SERVINGS
5-10 sticks

## INGREDIENTS

- Vegetable oil (as needed)
- Mozzarella cheese (1 block)
- Milk (2 tbsp.)
- Medium eggs (2)
- Breadcrumbs (1.5 cups)

**For Dipping:**

- Marinara sauce (as desired)

## DIRECTIONS

1. Slice the cheese into sticks. Whisk the eggs in one bowl with breadcrumbs and salt in another.
2. Dip each of the cheese sticks into the eggs, letting the excess drip away, and roll it in the breadcrumbs. Do this process twice and freeze them for a minimum of 1 hour.
3. Place the crisper basket in the Ninja and close the hood. Select the air fry mode set at 350° F/180° C. Push the start button to preheat.
4. Lightly spritz the frozen cheese sticks with vegetable oil.
5. Prepare them in small batches for 1 to 2 minutes. Occasionally shake the basket and serve promptly with marinara sauce.

# Veggie Egg Rolls

TIME REQUIRED

20 minutes

SERVINGS

4

## INGREDIENTS

- Eggplant (1)
- Chopped tomato (half of 1)
- Prepackaged egg roll wrappers
- Vegetable oil (for air fryer)
- Lime juice (1 lime)
- Fresh spinach (2 tbsp. - chopped)
- Garlic powder (1 tbsp.)
- Red onion (.25 cup - diced)
- Black pepper & salt (as desired)

## DIRECTIONS

1. Attach the Ninja crisper basket onto the unit and close the lid. Select the air fry function and push the start/stop button to begin preheating.
2. Dice and sauté the eggplant for a few minutes in a skillet. Mash it in a mixing container and add the rest of the fixings
3. Scoop the mixture into the egg roll wrapper. Roll it closed and lightly spritz it using a bit of vegetable cooking oil.
4. Prepare them in the fryer unit for 2 to 3 minutes, occasionally shaking for an even crisp.
5. Serve with your preferred dip.

# CHAPTER 12

## Advanced Snacks & Appetizers

# Foodi Grill Air Fryer - Taco Quesadillas

TIME REQUIRED

20-25 minutes

SERVINGS

**8**

## INGREDIENTS

**Cook in Advance:**

- Ground beef (1.5 lb./ 680g)
- Taco seasoning (as desired)
- Butter (2 tsp.)

**The Remainder of the Fixings:**

- Pico de Gallo or salsa (as desired)
- Corn or flou tortillas (8)
- Monterey Jack cheese - grated (12 oz./ 340g)
- Shredded lettuce (as desired)
- Sour cream (as desired)

## DIRECTIONS

1. Make the taco meat in advance (beef and taco seasoning) by warming the oil and butter to cook the beef. Fry it for about 15 minutes.
2. Insert the removable cooking pot and grill grate into the Ninja Foodi Grill.
3. Select the grill function, set time for 10 minutes (or longer if making multiple so you can skip reheating in between each time). Wait for about 8 minutes for it to preheat.
4. Once it signals to you to "Add Food," carefully place a tortilla with a handful of cheese over the top.
5. Place a tortilla on top and close the hood of the grill.
6. Wait for the cheese to thoroughly melt (around 6 min.). Then, add another handful of cheese on top.
7. Close the lid for a few minutes to allow it to melt.
8. Carefully remove and start topping the quesadilla by adding the topping with your favorite toppings.

# Granola Bites

TIME REQUIRED

30 minutes

SERVINGS

**4**

## INGREDIENTS

- Cooked vegetables (3 handfuls)
- Coconut milk (.25 cup)
- Coriander (1 tbsp.)
- Pepper & salt (as desired)
- Diced thyme (1 handful)
- Plain granola (3 oz.)

## DIRECTIONS

1. Place the crisper basket on the Ninja unit, setting it for 20 minutes at 350° F/180° C. Add the veggies to the granola.
2. Use an immersion blender to make a breadcrumb texture from the mixture.
3. Mix in the coconut milk to create a fir texture.
4. Make granola balls and place them onto the grill.
5. Cook for 20 minutes and serve.

# Gnocchi With Walnut & Sage Butter

TIME REQUIRED

15 minutes

SERVINGS

2

## INGREDIENTS

- Sunflowe oil (1 tbsp.)
- Gnocchi (10.5 oz./ 300g)
- Freshly grated hard cheese (0.35 oz./ 10g)
- Walnuts (0.7 oz./ 20g)
- Butter (1.1 oz./ 30g)
- Lemon juice (1 tbsp.)
- Sage leaves (6 - julienne cut)
- Garlic (1 clove)
- Salt & pepper (as desired)

## DIRECTIONS

1. Use a cooking pot without the grill plate or crisper basket installed on the Foodi. Close the hood and choose the roast setting at 360° F/180° C for 10 minutes. Press the start button to begin the preheat cycle.
2. After the Ninja beeps, it has preheated, so add the oil and gnocchi. Close lid to begin.
3. Mince the garlic. When there are 5 minutes left on the timer, open the hood and add butter, walnuts, garlic, sage, salt, and pepper. Stir and close the lid to continue cooking.
4. When ready, mix in the hard cheese and lemon juice. Serve promptly.

# Great Mac & Cheese Snack Bowl

TIME REQUIRED

20 minutes

SERVINGS

4

## INGREDIENTS

- Warm milk (.5 cup)
- Eggplant (1 @ 0.25 inch/ 0.6 cm thick)
- Grated parmesan cheese (1 tbsp.)
- Black pepper & salt (as desired)
- Grated cheddar cheese (1.5 cups)
- Elbow macaroni (1 cup)
- Broccoli (.5 cup)

## DIRECTIONS

1. Set the timer on the Ninja to 10 minutes at 400° F/ 200° C using the air crisp function. Push the start function to preheat the grill.
2. Meanwhile, boil the water and cook the veggies and macaroni for about 10 minutes. Drain them and combine them with the cheese and sauce. Season them with pepper and salt.
3. Sprinkle with cheese and close the hood to cook for 5 minutes. Flip them over (or not) and cook for another 10 minutes to serve.

# Ham & Cheese Noodle Casserole

TIME REQUIRED

30 minutes

SERVINGS

4

## INGREDIENTS

- Fine ribbon pasta (Feine Bandnudeln) – cooked (10.5 oz./ 300g)
- Ham - diced (7 oz./ 200g)
- Butter - diced (0.7 oz./ 20g)
- Milk (5.3 fl. oz./ 150ml)
- Eggs (4)
- Fresh parsley (1 tbsp.)
- Salt (1 tsp.)
- Nutmeg (.25 tsp.)
- Pepper (.5 tsp.)

## DIRECTIONS

1. Insert the Ninja cooking pot in the unit and close the hood. Choose the baking function at 360° F/180° C for 17 minutes. Push the start button to begin preheating.
2. Combine the cooked pasta with the ham, butter, and parsley. Thoroughly toss it to evenly distribute ham throughout the pasta.
3. Whisk the milk with the eggs, salt, pepper, and nutmeg. Whisk until it's thoroughly combined.
4. Once the unit has preheated, lightly spray the Ninja cooking pot with a spritz of cooking oil spray. Add the pasta to the pot, and pour in the egg mixture. Close hood to begin cooking.
5. When ready, remove the pot to the countertop to cool slightly. Serve as a snack, main or side dish.

# Seared Tuna Salad

TIME REQUIRED

16 minutes

SERVINGS

4

## INGREDIENTS

- Ahi tuna (4 @ 1.8 oz./ 50g each strip)
- Sesame oil (2 tbsp.)
- Baby greens (10 oz./ 280g)
- Rice wine vinegar (2 tbsp.)
- Extra-virgin olive oil (6 tbsp.)
- English cucumber - sliced (½)
- Sea salt (0.25 tsp.)
- Black pepper (½ tsp.)

## DIRECTIONS

1. Supplement the flame broil mesh and close the hood.
2. Preheat Ninja Foodi by pressing the "Grill" option at and setting it to "Max" and timer to 6 minutes.
3. Take a small bowl, whisk together the rice vinegar, salt, and pepper.
4. Slowly pour in the oil while whisking until vinaigrette is fully combined.
5. Season the fish with salt and pepper, sprinkle with the sesame oil.
6. Once it preheats until you hear a beep.
7. Arrange the shrimp over the grill grate lock lid and cook for 6 minutes.
8. Do not flip during cooking.
9. Once cooked completely, top salad with tuna strip.
10. Drizzle the vinaigrette over the top.
11. Serve immediately and enjoy!

# Italian Basil Pizza

TIME REQUIRED

27 minutes

SERVINGS

4

## INGREDIENTS

- Olive oil (.25 cup)
- Sliced sausage (4 @ 4 oz./ 115g each)
- Tomato basil paste (1 cup)
- Grated parmesan cheese (.5 cup)
- Bread pieces (4 flat
- Mozzarella shredded cheese (2 cups)
- Thinly sliced basil (.5 cup)

## DIRECTIONS

1. Warm the Foodi grill using the high setting for 12 minutes. Push the start button and wait for the beep. It is ready to add the sliced sauce to the grill grids.
2. Grill about 3 minutes per side. Also, grill the bread 3 minutes after it's lightly oiled.
3. Top the bread with the sausage, cheese, basil, and sauce.
4. Place the bread on the heated grill to bake on low for 5 minutes and serve.

# Personal-Size Grilled Pizza

TIME REQUIRED

24 minutes

SERVINGS

**2**

## INGREDIENTS

- All-purpose flou (2 tbsp. + more as needed)
- Store-bought pizza dough (1 @ 6 oz./ 170g pkg.)
- Canola oil, divided (1 tbsp.)
- Pizza or alfredo sauce (.5 cup)
- Ricotta cheese (.5 cup)
- Shredded mozzarella cheese (1 cup)
- Pepperoni (12–15 slices)

**Optional to serve:**

- Dried oregano

## DIRECTIONS

1. Place the grill grate in the Ninja unit and close the hood.
2. Choose the grill function to max heat for 7 minutes.
3. Push the start/stop button to begin preheating.
4. In the meantime, spread the flou over a clean work surface, such as a cutting board.
5. Use a rolling pin to flatte the dough on the floure surface, adding additional flou as needed to ensure the dough does not stick to the rolling pin (no larger than 9 inch/ 23 cm across, so it will fi on the grill grate).
6. Brush the surface with ½ tablespoon of oil. Flip the dough over and brush with remaining oil (½ tbsp.). Poke the dough with a fork fiv or six times across its surface to prevent air pockets from forming as it cooks.
7. Once it has preheated, place the dough on the grill grate. Close the hood and cook for 4 minutes.
8. At that point, fli the dough, and cover it using the sauce. Sprinkle with cheese and pepperoni slices, if desired.
9. Close the lid and continue cooking for the remaining 2 minutes, or until the cheese is melted and pepperoni slices begin to crisp.
10. When ready, cool slightly and top with dried oregano as desired before slicing.

# Pesto & Goat's Cheese Flatbread

TIME REQUIRED

16 minutes

SERVINGS

4

## INGREDIENTS

- Ready to use pizza dough (1)
- Pesto (3 tbsp.)
- Goat's cheese - crumbled (1.4 oz./ 40g)
- Parmesan - finel grated (1 oz./ 30g)
- Sun-dried tomatoes (1 oz./ 30g)
- Freshly chopped basil

**To Finish:**

- Olive oil -brushing & drizzling
- Salt & freshly cracked black pepper (as desired)

## DIRECTIONS

1. Position the grill plate in the unit and close the hood.
2. Choose the grill function and set it using the high-temperature setting for 2 minutes. Preheat using the start/stop function.
3. Roll out the pizza dough and pierce it lightly with a fork to prevent too many air bubbles while baking.
4. Wait for the beep signifying it has preheated, arrange the rolled dough on top of the grill plate, close the lid, and set a timer for 2 minutes.
5. When there's 1 minute left on the timer - fli the dough.
6. When the cooking process is complete, remove the flatbrea from the Ninja and set it to the side.
7. Leave the grill plate in the unit, choosing the grill setting. Set the temperature using the high setting for 4 minutes. Hit "start-stop" to preheat.
8. Lightly brush edges of flatbrea with olive oil. Spread the pesto over the top, leaving about 0.4 inch/ 1 cm around the edges. Sprinkle with goat's cheese and parmesan.
9. When you hear the beep, it signifie it has preheated, open the lid and arrange the flatbrea on the grill plate. Close the hood and allow it to cook.
10. When it beeps, remove flatbrea from the unit. Place it onto a cutting board and dress with dried tomatoes, freshly cut basil, and freshly ground salt and pepper. Lightly drizzle with olive oil and serve promptly.

# Pizza Snails

TIME REQUIRED
25 minutes

SERVINGS
4

## INGREDIENTS

- Ready to use pizza dough (1)
- Mozzarella - grated (6 oz./170g)
- Ham (5 slices)
- Tomato passata (7 oz./ 200g)
- Oregano (1 tsp.)
- Pepper & Salt
- Basil (1 tsp.)
- Oil (1 tbsp.)

**Toppings:**

- Sour cream (as desired)
- Chives (as desired)

## DIRECTIONS

1. Whisk the tomato passata with the oregano, basil, oil, pepper, and salt.
2. Put the cooking pot on the grill and select the bake mode.
3. Set temperature to 390° F/ 200° C, and set the timer to 10 minutes. Push the "start-stop" to begin preheating.
4. Roll out the pizza dough and evenly spread tomato sauce over its surface, leaving a 0.8 inch/ 2 cm edge.
5. Cover the dough with ½ of the mozzarella, then top with ham, and sprinkle again with the rest of the cheese.
6. Roll the dough with its toppings quite tightly into a roll, leaving the clear edge. Lightly brush the edge with water to make sure it sticks well and close the roll. Cut the pizza roll into 0.8 inch/ 2 cm wide slices.
7. Once the unit has beeped to trigger you that it's preheated, line the crisper basket with baking paper, and add in half of the pizza slices.
8. Open the lid, add the crisper basket to the unit, and close the lid to begin cooking.
   Once cocking has been completed, remove the pizza snails and repeat steps two and six.
9. Serve hot and garnish as desired.

# Sea Salt Focaccia

TIME REQUIRED
35 minutes
+ proo ng time (8 hours)

SERVINGS
**8**

## INGREDIENTS

- Strong plain flou (12.5 oz./ 350g)
- Dried yeast (1 tsp.)
- Fine-grain sea salt (1.25 tsp.)
- Olive oil - divided (3 tbsp. + extra for greasing)
- Water (8 fl. oz./ 225 ml)
- White wine or use all water (2.2 fl. oz./ 60 ml)
- A pinch of Flaked sea salt
- For the Grill & Air Fryer - AG551
- Strong plain flou (14 oz./ 400g)
- Fast-action/easy bake yeast (1 sachet)
- Salt (1.25 tsp.)
- Olive oil - divided (3 tbsp.)
- Tepid water (8.75-10.5 fl oz./ 250-300 ml)
- Flaked sea salt - for sprinkling

## DIRECTIONS

1. Whisk the flou with the yeast, sea salt, two tablespoons olive oil, water, and wine in a mixing container. Mix it roughly with a one-handed kneading action for about 1 to 2 minutes, ensuring that everything is thoroughly combined. The dough will be sticky.
2. Cover the bowl with a plastic cling fil and pop it in the fridge to prove for a minimum of 8 hours or up to 24 hours. (For the quick method, proof it at room temperature for about 2 hours or until doubled in size.)
3. Take the dough out of the fridge about 2 hours before you plan to bake the focaccia.
4. Line the crisping basket with a sheet of parchment baking paper coming about 2 inch/ 5 cm up the sides. Oil the parchment lightly with your hands. Arrange the dough in the crisping basket, spreading it out roughly to the corners. (It will continue to spread and fil the basket as it proofs).
5. Cover the crisping basket with cling fil and let it proof at room temperature for a minimum of 2-2.5 hours. (If you have chosen the quicker proving method, the second proof will be about half an hour or until doubled in volume).
6. When you are ready to bake the focaccia, mix the remaining one tablespoon of olive oil with one tablespoon of water and drizzle it over the focaccia's surface. Use both hands to dimple the dough all over the surface by digging the fingertip into the mix. Sprinkle it using sea salt flake and any additional toppings of choice.
7. Close the hood and choose the bake setting for 25 minutes at 375° F/ 190° C. Push the start button to begin preheating.
8. When the unit beeps to signify it has preheated, arrange the crisping basket into the pot and close the hood. Check the focaccia after about 18 minutes. It should sound hollow when tapped if cooked and should be nicely browned on top. When the focaccia is cooked, carefully lift the crisping basket out of the unit and remove the focaccia from the baking parchment.
9. Transfer the focaccia onto a cooling rack, removing the parchment from under it. Allow cooling before eating.

# CHAPTER 13

## Dehydrator Favorites

Most temperatures used with a dehydrator are between 135° F/ 55° C up to 165° F/ 75° C. Times may vary depending on the texture you are looking to achieve and how you slice or dice.

# Ninja Foodi Spicy Watermelon

TIME REQUIRED

12 hours

SERVINGS

1 cup

## INGREDIENTS

- Seedless watermelon (2 cups @ 1 inch/ 2.5 cm) cubes

## DIRECTIONS

1. Arrange the watermelon cubes in a single layer in the cook & crisp basket. Place the basket in the cooker and close the crisping hood.
2. Press the dehydrate function with the temperature to 135° F/55° C for 12 hours.
3. Hit the start button to begin.
4. When dehydrating is complete, remove the basket from the pot and transfer the jerky to an airtight container.

These are perfectly safe for your pet!

# Beef Jerky

TIME REQUIRED

6 hours

SERVINGS

Varies 2lb./ 900g

## INGREDIENTS

- Lean-cut of beef - ex. round, bottom, or flan  steak (2 lb./ 900g - sliced)

**Equipment you Need:**

Ninja Foodi

Ninja Foodi Grill

## DIRECTIONS

1. Slice the beef into thin, even strips. Set on the dehydrator rack, be sure the meat is not touching.
2. Set the Foodi to 135° F/55° C for 6 hours.
3. Share with our favorite puppy!

# Chicken Jerky

TIME REQUIRED

4 hours 5 minutes

SERVINGS

Varies

## INGREDIENTS

- Boneless chicken (3 lb./ 1.4 kg)

## DIRECTIONS

1. Slice the chicken into ¼ inch/ 0.7 cm slices.
2. Arrange them in a single layer in the Foodi Dehydrator racks.
3. Place on the dehydrate function at 165° F/75° C for 4 hours.

# Dehydrated Apples

TIME REQUIRED

8 hours

SERVINGS

Varies

## INGREDIENTS

- Apples Granny Smith Apples or McIntosh (2.5 lb./ 1.1 kg)
- Cinnamon (1.5 tsp.)

**Equipment you Need:**

Ninja Foodi

Dehydrator

Ninja Foodi Grill

## DIRECTIONS

1. Wash, peel, and core the apples.
2. Thinly slice apples at about ¼ inch/ 0.7 cm.
3. Layer the sliced rings on the dehydrator wire rack. Be sure to leave a small amount of space around each slice to allow air to circulate.
4. Lightly sprinkle the apple slices with a dusting of cinnamon.
5. Set the dehydrate mode at 135° F/55° C for 6 to 8 hours, checking at the 6 hour mark. Close the hood and continue to dry depending on the desired texture.
6. Check, both inside and outside of rings; ideal slices will feel dry and leathery without being sticky.
7. Tear an apple slice in half to check for moisture inside; it should resemble a dry sponge-like texture.
8. Once done, cool for several hours and store in an airtight bag or container – make sure they are entirely cool to not create any moisture.
9. Let your four-legged baby be the taste tester, and then, of course, you enjoy a slice too.

# Dehydrated Sweet Potatoes

TIME REQUIRED

7 hours

SERVINGS

varies

## INGREDIENTS

- Sweet Potatoes (4 medium - similar size)

**Equipment you Need:**

Ninja Foodi

Ninja Foodi Grill

Dehydrator

## DIRECTIONS

1. Thoroughly wash and peel the potatoes. Slice it into ¼ inch/ 0.7 cm thin slices
2. Arrange them on the dehydrator rack - not touching - allowing space for air to flow
3. Dehydrate for 6 to 8 hours at 150° F/ 70° C – crunchier treats may take a little longer.
4. Cool and store in an airtight glass container placed in a cool, dark place. They can be stored for up to 2 months, but they won't last but a few days!

**NOTE:** Green beans can also be done and make for a great snack. Rinse, pat dry, and set the rack apart at 165° F/75° C for about 7 hours.

# CHAPTER 14

## Easy Dessert Favorites

# Caramelized Mango Spears

TIME REQUIRED

20 minutes

SERVINGS

3

## INGREDIENTS

- Honey (.5 cup)
- Unsalted liquid butter (.5 cup)
- Brown sugar (1 cup)
- Mango spears (1 whole)

## DIRECTIONS

1. Place the Ninja grate on the grill unit and close the hood. Set the function to "Grill" at the "Max" setting for 10 minutes. Push the start button to begin the preheat cycle.
2. Whisk all of the fixing  (omit the mango) and heat until it's a little 'runny.'
3. When the preheat buzzer sounds, place the mango on the grill, adding the liquid mixture.
4. Close the lid and cook for 5 minutes. Open the top, turn the pineapple, and close the hood for the last 5 minutes.
5. Cool it slightly before serving.

# Biscoff Brownies

TIME REQUIRED

45 minutes

SERVINGS

**8**

## INGREDIENTS

- Unsalted butter (7.4 oz./210g)
- Dark chocolate (7.4 oz. - chopped/ 210g)
- Eggs (3)
- Caster sugar (9.7 oz./275g)
- Plain flou (5.3 oz./150g)
- Biscoff Biscuits (1.4 oz./40g - broken in uneven pieces)
- Biscoff Spread (2.6 oz./75g)
- Salted caramel (2-3 tbsp.)

## DIRECTIONS

1. Warm the Foodi grill to 300°F/150° C.
2. Spray a disposable 8 inch/ 20 cm foil container with cooking spray.
3. Set a bowl over a pot of water (make sure the bowl's bottom is not touching the water). Add the chocolate and butter to melt using the low-temperature setting. Transfer the bowl from heat and set aside.
4. Once slightly cooled, add the eggs and sugar. Whisk for 3 to 5 minutes. Fold in the flour Fold in the Biscoff biscuits and pour into the container.
5. Add blobs of the Bischoff spread on top of the brownie batter and swirl in with a cocktail stick.
6. Bake for 30 to 35 minutes. Remove from the Ninja unit and drizzle it using caramel and more Biscoff biscuits.

# Lebkuchen Cake

TIME REQUIRED
35 minutes

SERVINGS
**9**

## INGREDIENTS

- Plain flou  (12.3 oz./350g)
- Caster sugar (6 oz./170g)
- Vanilla extract (1 tsp.)
- Cocoa powder (2 tbsp.)
- Nutmeg (.25 tsp.)
- Baking powder (1 tsp.)
- Cinnamon (1 tsp.)
- Ginger powder (.5 tsp.)
- Allspice (.25 tsp.)
- Clove (.25 tsp.)
- Eggs (3)
- Oil (3.5 fl  oz./200 ml)
- Milk (3.5 fl  oz./100 ml)

**For Greasing:**

- Cooking spray

## DIRECTIONS

1. Measure and toss each of the dry fixing  into a mixing container. Whisk and add in the eggs, oil, and milk. Mix until it's thoroughly combined.
2. Use the cooking pot without the grill plate or basket installed. Close the hood and choose the bake function at 340° F/170° C for 30 minutes. Push the start/stop button to begin preheating.
3. When you hear the beep, it's preheated. Open the hood and lightly grease the pot with a spritz of cooking oil spray or line with parchment baking paper.
4. Empty the cake mixture into the pot and close the lid to begin cooking.
5. After ½ hour, check whether the cake is done. Check it with a wooden skewer inserted in the center of the cake. If it comes out clean, carefully remove the cooking pot, and let the cake slightly cool.
6. Serve chilled or warm.

# No-Flour Honey & Peanut Butter Cookies

TIME REQUIRED

25 minutes

SERVINGS

12 cookies

## INGREDIENTS

- Egg (1)
- Peanut butter (.5 cup)
- Honey (.5 cup)

## DIRECTIONS

1. Set the Foodi grill to the bake setting at 300° F/150° C. Choose the start button to begin the preheat cycle.
2. Whisk the fixing and roll a tablespoon of the dough. Flatten it into cookies. When the unit beeps, open the hood and cook for about 5 to 6 minutes and check for doneness. Bake until they are golden brown.

# Mini Brownies

TIME REQUIRED

20 minutes

SERVINGS

**2**

## INGREDIENTS

- Eggs (2 large)
- Unsalted butter (1 stick)
- Honey (1 cup)
- Flour (.5 cup)
- Chocolate chips (2 cups )
- Salt (1 sprinkle)

**Optional:**

- Vanilla ice cream

## DIRECTIONS

1. Prepare the Ninja grill by setting it to the bake function at 300° F/150° C. Push the start button to preheat the unit. Set the time for 10 minutes.
2. Cream the honey with the butter and mix in the eggs. Fill in the chips, salt, and flour
3. Put the dough on the baking tray to cook for 10 minutes. Serve as desired.

# Pear Fritters

TIME REQUIRED

35 minutes

SERVINGS

**6**

## INGREDIENTS

- Ground cinnamon (.5 tsp.)
- Milk (1/3 cup)
- Salt (.5 tsp.)
- Brown sugar (1 tbsp.)
- Honey (.5 cup)
- Pears (2)
- Large egg (1)
- Vegetable oil (as needed)
- Flour (.5 cup)

## DIRECTIONS

1. Rinse and peel the pears. Finely chop the pears.
2. Arrange the Foodi crisper basket to the Ninja grill unit and close the hood.
3. Select the air fry function and push the start button to begin preheating.
4. Sift the flour and dry fixings. Whisk the eggs with the honey and fold them into the dry components. Work in the pears.
5. Lightly spritz the mixture with oil for a crispier dish.
6. Cook using ¼ of the batter in the basket, shaking for even crisping.
7. Dip the fritters into the prepared glaze and let them set to serve promptly.

# Rum Sundae

TIME REQUIRED

18 minutes

SERVINGS

**4**

## INGREDIENTS

- Pineapple (1)
- Ground cinnamon (1 tsp.)
- Packed brown sugar (.5 cup)
- Dark rum (.5 cup)

**To serve:**

- Vanilla ice cream

## DIRECTIONS

1. Remove the core and slice the pineapple.
2. Pour the rum, sugar, and cinnamon into a large mixing container.
3. Add the pineapple and dredge it through the mixture.
4. Set the "Grill" to preheat by pushing the start button with the unit set for 8 minutes using the "Max" setting.
5. After the preheated beep sounds, strain the juices from the slices and place them on the grill. Press them to achieve grill marks and cook for 6 to 8 minutes. Do not overcrowd, so cook in batches if necessary.
6. When ready to serve, add a scoop of ice cream and a bit of cinnamon.

# CHAPTER 15

## Advanced Desserts

# Apple Strudel

TIME REQUIRED

40 minutes

SERVINGS

4

## INGREDIENTS

- Lemon juice (1 tbsp.)
- Apples (4)
- Brown sugar (1.4 oz./ 40g)
- Cinnamon (.5 tsp.)
- Nutmeg (.25 tsp.)
- Raisins (2.1 oz./ 60g)
- Brown sugar (1.4 oz./ 40g)
- Ready-rolled puff pastry (9.7 oz./ 275g)
- Egg for brushing (1)
- Breadcrumbs (2 tbsp.)

**Optional Toppings:**

- Vanilla sauce
- A favorite ice cream

## DIRECTIONS

1. Peel and grate the apples into a sieve with a spritz of lemon juice. Lightly squeeze to remove excess juice from the apples. Arrange them in a big mixing container with the sugar, raisins, cinnamon, and nutmeg. Mix well.
2. Insert the Ninja pot in the unit and close the hood. Select the bake function at 340° F/ 170°C and set timer to 25 minutes. Press the “start/stop” to start preheating.
3. Meanwhile, spread the puff pastry out, sprinkle the center using breadcrumbs to help absorb juices from the apples during baking. Arrange the apple mixture down the middle over the breadcrumbs.
4. Cut the sides of the pastry into approximately 0.4 inch/ 1 cm wide strips. Beginning at the top, fold the left strip at a 45° angle over the apple mixture. Then do the same with the right strip. Continue the process until you have plated all the strips and tuck the bottom strips sticking out underneath the strudel.
5. Once the unit beeps to signify it is preheated, line the pot with baking paper, and place strudel in the pot diagonally. Close the hood and cook for 10 minutes.
6. Whisk the egg in a cup. Once there are 10 minutes left on the timer, open the top and brush the strudel with the egg. Close the hood and continue cooking.
7. When ready, carefully remove the strudel from the unit and let it cool.
8. Serve as desired with your favorite toppings.

# Beetroot & Tarragon Souffle

TIME REQUIRED

20 minutes

SERVINGS

2

## INGREDIENTS

- Boiled beetroot (7 oz./ 200g)
- Chopped fresh tarragon leaves (2 tbsp.) or Dried tarragon (1 tbsp.)
- Sea salt (.25 to .5 tsp.)
- Black pepper (.25 tsp.)
- Milk (2.7 fl oz./ 80 ml)
- Rice flou (0.5 oz./15g)
- Eggs (2 - separated)
- Cream of tartar (1 pinch)

**For Greasing:**

- Melted butter (0.35 oz./ 10g)

**For Dusting:**

- Gluten-free fin breadcrumbs or rice flou (0.35 oz./10g)
- Coconut or plain yogurt (3.5 oz./100g)
- Fresh lemon juice (2 tbsp.)
- 1 lemon zest
- Creamed horseradish (1 tbsp.)

## DIRECTIONS

1. Remove the skin from the beetroot and combine it in a blender with the freshly chopped/dried tarragon, sea salt, and black pepper. Mix in half the milk and blend until smooth.
2. Warm the milk in a pan until it comes to a boil. Transfer the pan from the burner and whisk in the flou until smooth. Cool it slightly and add it to the blender. Whirl it again until it's creamy smooth.
3. Mix in the egg yolks one at a time, mix again, and pour the mixture into a large mixing container.
4. Place the crisper basket into the Ninja unit, and pre-heat to 390° F/200° C. Set the time to 10 minutes. Grease and dust the ramekins and set them to one side.
5. Whisk the egg whites in a stand mixer until stif Using a metal spoon, gently fold into the beetroot mixture until the mixture is incorporated.
6. Transfer the mixture into the dusted ramekins. Put them into the Ninja grill and close the hood.
7. Whisk the fixing for the horseradish and lemon yogurt and set to one side.
8. Once the cooking cycle is complete, remove it, and serve immediately.

# Chocolate Souffle For Two

TIME REQUIRED

28 minutes

SERVINGS

2

## INGREDIENTS

- Butter (2.1 oz./ 60g)
- Caster sugar (1.75 oz./ 50g)
- Chocolate - chopped (3.2 oz./ 90g)
- Eggs (2 separated)
- Vanilla extract (.5 tsp.)
- Plain flou (0.9 oz./25g)
- Salt (a pinch)

**To Serve:**

- Icing sugar
- Whipped cream

## DIRECTIONS

1. Prepare two 7 fl. oz./ 200ml ramekins. Butter the inside surfaces, dusting with sugar, shaking it around to remove any excess.
2. Use a microwave-safe bowl to combine the butter with the chocolate. Melt it using ½ minute increments, stirring after each cook time until well melted and combined.
3. Use an electric mixer to whisk the egg whites into the soft peak stage (the whites will almost stand up on the end of your whisk).
4. Insert the crisper basket to the Ninja and close the hood.
5. Choose the air fry mode and set the temperature at 320° F/ 160° C. Press "Start-Stop" to begin the preheating stage.
6. Whisk the yolks of the egg with the vanilla and sugar. While whisking, slowly empty the chocolate-butter mixture into the egg yolks. Continue whisking until thoroughly combined.
7. Sift in the flou and salt until so lumps are removed.
8. Fold 1/3 of the egg whites into the batter. Slowly mix in the rest of the whites until thoroughly mixed.
9. Transfer the light and airy batter carefully to the prepared ramekins, leaving 0.4-0.8 inch/ 1-2 cm of room at the top. Note: The souffl will puff above the edge of the ramekins but will not overflow
10. When the unit beeps to signify it has preheated, insert the ramekins into the Ninja. Close the lid and set the cooking time for 13 minutes.
11. When it beeps, open the hood and slightly cool the soufflé Use tongs to carefully remove the soufflé dishes to a plate or wire rack.
12. Dust with icing sugar, or top with whipped cream, and serve promptly.

# Grilled Apple & Raspberry Pie

TIME REQUIRED

1 hour 30 minutes

SERVINGS

**8**

## INGREDIENTS

- Juice of 1 lemon
- Cold water (8 cups)
- Granny Smith apples (8)
- Raspberries (1.5 cups)
- Dark brown & granulated sugar - divided (.25 cup + 1 tbsp. each)
- Ground ginger (.5 tsp.)
- Ground cinnamon (.5 tsp.)
- All-purpose flou (3 tbsp.)
- Applesauce (.5 cup)
- Frozen pie crust (1 defrosted)

**Optional to Serve:**

- Ice cream

## DIRECTIONS

1. Peel, remove the cores, and slice the apples into quarters. Rinse the raspberries and juice the lemon.
2. Whisk the lemon juice with the water and apple slices in a mixing container. Let the pieces soak for about 10 minutes. Remove them from the water and pat until dry.
3. Insert the grill grate in the Foodi unit and close the top.
4. Choose the "Grill" mode at "Max" temperature for 8 minutes. Push in the start button to begin preheating.
5. Meanwhile, dice eight of the apple slices and set them aside. In another mixing container, toss the rest of the sliced apples with one tablespoon dark brown sugar and one tablespoon granulated sugar until they're evenly coated.
6. When the unit beeps to signify it has preheated, arrange the slices tossed with sugar on the grill grate and cook for 8 minutes. Don't fli slices during grilling.
7. Combine the raspberries with the rest of the dark brown sugar, remaining granulated sugar, ginger, applesauce, cinnamon, flour and diced apples in a mixing container.
8. When cooking is complete, gently fold the grilled apples into the combined fixing in the mixing bowl.
9. Pour mixture into the Ninja multi-purpose pan (8 inch/ 20 cm baking pan), spreading evenly. Lay the pie crust over the top and pinch around the edges to ensure it adheres to the pan. Using a knife, cut several Xs in the dough, so steam can escape during baking.
10. Remove the grill grate from the Foodi unit. Choose the bake setting, set the temperature to 350° F/ 180° C, and set the timer for 20 minutes. Push the start button to begin preheating.
11. When the unit beeps to signify it has preheated, arrange the pan directly in the Foodi, close the hood, and cook for 20 minutes.
12. When it's ready, let it cool for 20 minutes before serving warm with ice cream or as desired.

# Grilled Strawberry Shortcake Skewers

TIME REQUIRED

1 hour 6 minutes

SERVINGS

5

## INGREDIENTS

- Classic white cake mix (1 box)
- Optional: Premade vanilla pudding (1 cup)
- Cooking oil spray (as needed)
- Strawberries (2 cups)
- Granulated sugar (.25 cup)
- Honey (2 tbsp.)
- Skewers (5)

**To serve:**

- Whipped cream
- Vanilla ice cream

**Also needed:**

- Ninja multi-purpose pan or an 8 inch/ 20 cm baking pan

## DIRECTIONS

1. Mix the cake batter according to the instructions on the box. A second option to use is to substitute the one cup of water with one cup premade vanilla pudding for a cake that is denser and better able to stand up to high-temperature grilling.
2. Remove the grill grate from the unit and close the hood.
3. Choose the Bake function with the temperature-setting to 325° F/165° C. Set the timer for 40 minutes. Hit the stop/ start to preheat.
4. While the unit is preheating, generously coat the multi-purpose pan with a spritz of cooking oil spray. Pour batter into the pan.
5. When the unit has beeps to signify it has preheated, arrange the pan in the pot. Shut the hood to cook for 40 minutes.
6. Meanwhile, prepare the berries by cutting them into halves and removing the stems. Put the strawberries in a mixing container. Toss them with sugar until well coated. Let them sit for 5 to 10 minutes. Stir in the honey - mixing well to coat. Set the berries to the side for now.
7. When cooking is complete, cake the cake for 15 to 20 minutes, remove it from the pan, and use a serrated knife to cut it into 2x2 inch/ 5x5 cm cubes. Assemble the skewers alternating between berries and the cake cubes. Reserve the liquid from the berries.
8. Insert the grill grate in the unit and close the hood.
9. Choose the "Grill" mode, setting the temperature at high. Set the timer for 6 minutes. Select "Start/Stop" to start preheating.
10. While the unit is preheating, spray each skewer using cooking spray.
11. When the unit has beeps, arrange the skewers on the grill grate. Shut the hood and cook for 3 minutes.
12. Flip the skewers over, close the hood, and continue cooking for another 3 minutes.
13. Once they're done, transfer the skewers to a serving platter. Spoon the strawberry juices over the top and garnish as desired to serve.

# Persimmon Pomegranate Eton Mess Cake

TIME REQUIRED

50 minutes

SERVINGS

**8**

## INGREDIENTS

- Eggs (3 whole + 1 yolk)
- Caster sugar (3.5 oz./ 100g)
- Vanilla extract (.5 tsp.)
- Plain flou  (3.2 oz./ 90g)
- Baking powder (.25 tsp.)
- Bicarbonate of soda (.25 tsp.)
- Salt (1 pinch)
- Lemon juice (1 tsp.)
- Rapeseed oil (2.6 fl  oz./ 75 ml)

**The Whipped Cream:**

- Double - whipping cream (17.5 fl  oz./ 500 ml)
- Caster sugar (1.7 oz./ 50g)
- Vanilla extract (1 tsp.)

**The Toppings:**

- Pomegranate (1 - seeds removed) or Fresh pomegranate seeds (1.7 oz./ 50 g)
- Persimmons - aka Sharon fruit (3 ripe)
- Meringue shells (1 pack)

**Also Needed:**

- 7 inch/ 18 cm springform cake tin

## DIRECTIONS

1. Select the bake function and set the temperature to 340° F/ 170° C. Hit the start button to begin preheating. Grease and line the cake tin.
2. Break and add the whole eggs, yolk, vanilla, and sugar in the bowl of an electric mixer fitte with a whisk attachment. Whisk on high for 5 to 10 minutes until the batter is pale or reaches a "thick ribbon" stage. (Pull the whisk straight out of the bowl, the batter will fall back into the bowl in thick ribbons.)
3. In another container, sift the flou with the baking powder, salt, and bicarbonate of soda. Sprinkle the dry ingredients over the fluffy egg mixture and fold until just combined.
4. Mix in the lemon juice and oil until just combined.
5. When the unit beeps, insert the springform tin into the Foodi unit. Close the hood and set the timer for ½ hour.
6. When cook time is finished check the cake is baked. A skewer should come out clean from the center of the cake. If needed, cook for an additional 5 minutes. Transfer the cake to a cooling rack.
7. Meanwhile, make the whipped cream. Pour the double cream into the bowl of the electric mixer. Whisk it using the med-high setting until slightly thickened, and gradually add in the sugar and vanilla.
8. Whisk on high until soft peaks form. Set it aside.
9. Insert the grill plate into the Ninja unit and close the hood. Choose the grill setting on the high temperature setting. Push the start button to begin preheating.
10. While the Foodi unit is preheating, using a sharp knife, cut the persimmons into approx. 0.2-0.4 inch/ 0.5-1 cm thick slices.
11. When it has preheated, open the hood and gently brush or spray the grill plate using a small amount of oil.
12. Layer the persimmon slices onto the grill in a single layer. Close the lid and set the timer for 3 minutes.
13. At that time, use silicone tongs to remove the grilled persimmon slices. Place them on a plate or sheet of parchment to cool.
14. Repeat this procedure until you have grilled all of the persimmon slices. Set aside some beautiful slices for the top of your cake, then cut or rip the rest of the slices into small chunks.
15. Assemble the cake: Release the cake from the tin, removing it from the base as well. Use a thin palette knife to release the cake from the pan edges and bottom as needed. Use a large serrated knife to cut the cake horizontally into three equal slices.
16. Place the bottom layer onto a cake plate, and spread with a layer of whipped cream. Push small or broken up pieces of meringue shell into the whipped cream, then layer on slices of persimmon, and sprinkle on pomegranate seeds.
17. Repeat this process with the second layer of cake by placing the top layer of the cake, and decorate as desired with the remaining whipped cream, meringue cookies, persimmon slices, and pomegranate seeds.
18. Note: This cake is best made and served on the same day, as the crunchy meringue will soften over time or if placed in the fridge.

# Profiteroles

TIME REQUIRED

1 hours

SERVINGS

**10**

## INGREDIENTS

- Milk - nut or cows (5.3 oz./ 150 ml)
- Unsalted butter - cubed (2.1 oz./ 60g)
- Sea salt - fine-grin (1 pinch/as desired)
- Coconut sugar (1 tbsp.)
- Vanilla extract (1 tsp.)
- Medium eggs (2)
- Tapioca flou (4.8 oz./ 135g)
- Coconut flou (1 tbsp.)
- Baking powder (.5 tsp.)
- The Whipped Coconut Cream:
- Coconut milk - full-fat - refrigerated overnight - 2 cans @ 14 oz./ 400ml each)
- Vanilla extract (1 tsp.)
- Maple syrup or agave nectar (1 tbsp.)

**The Glaze:**

- High-quality dark chocolate - at least 70% cacao solids (3.5 oz./ 100g)
- Unsalted butter (0.9 oz./ 25g)

## DIRECTIONS

1. Boil the milk with the butter, coconut sugar, vanilla, and sea salt in a saucepan.
2. Gather the dry fixing in a mixing container. Remove the pan from the burner and whisk in the coconut flour baking powder, and tapioca flou rapidly with a wooden spoon until smooth. Work quickly, or the mixture can become lumpy. It should come away from the sides and form a nice 'ball' of choux dough. If not, place it back over the burner using the low-temperature setting and simmer until it does, stirring continuously. Cool the mixture for a few minutes.
3. Whisk one egg, then beat into the mixture; if needed, whisk in the second egg and carefully add a teaspoon at a time. The mixture should reluctantly fall from the spoon. It should be stiff and not runny when you prod a wet finge into the dough; it should leave a dent. If your mixture becomes lumpy, run it through a food processor on low until well combined.
4. Place a round piping tip into a piping bag. Fill the piping bag with the dough, push out any air, and twist the end. Place the piping bag into the refrigerator until needed.
5. Attach the air fryer basket into the pot of your Ninja Grill & Air Fryer. Close the lid and press Air Fry at 340° F/170° C for 13 minutes. Wait for the unit to pre-heat.
6. When ready, remove the piping bag from the refrigerator and pipe fiv circles carefully into the basket (1 inch/ 2.5 cm apart and about 2 inch/ 5 cm in diameter). Using a wet finger gently press down any bumps. Close the lid and return the piping bag to the fridge.
7. After 10 minutes, open the hood and pierce each choux bun with a skewer.
8. Shut the hood and cook for another 3 minutes. Remove the basket with oven mitts, then leave to cool for a couple minutes.
9. Lift the basket and, using the back of a wooden spoon, knock the bottom where any dough has cooked through the basket. This will release them from the basket. Pierce the choux buns again and leave to cool on a wire rack.
10. Repeat the process for the remaining dough.
11. Prepare the whipped coconut cream. Remove the cans of chilled coconut milk from the fridge. Open the cans, poke a hole into the creamy top layer, and drain out all of the water. Scoop out all of the solid cream into a large mixing bowl.
12. Add the rest of the fixing into the cream and whisk using broad strokes to beat in as much air as possible to make the cream fluffy and light. Once the cream forms large stiff peaks, it is done. Transfer into piping bags and use a large round or star tipped nozzle.
13. For the glaze, place the chocolate into a double boiler using the low-temperature setting until melted. Add the butter and stir until smooth.
14. Take the whipped cream and insert the piping tip into the bottom of the profiterole Pipe in the cream until full. Alternatively, slice the bun in half and then spoon in some cream, then place the lid on top. Repeat until all buns have been filled
15. Either dip each bun into the glaze or assemble onto a plate and drizzle all over. Sprinkle over a little gold luster dust for decoration if you wish Serve promptly.

# Quark Schmarrn

TIME REQUIRED

18 minutes

SERVINGS

**3**

## INGREDIENTS

- Eggs (4 - separate whites & yolks)
- Caster sugar (2.5 oz./ 70g)
- Salt (.25 tsp.)
- Milk (3.5 oz./ 100g)
- Quark - dairy (8.8 oz./ 250g)
- Plain flou (5.3 oz./ 150g)
- Butter (0.35 oz./ 10g)

**For Dusting:**

- Icing sugar

## DIRECTIONS

1. Whisk the egg whites to make stiff peaks and set to the side for now.
2. Insert the cooking pot into the Ninja unit and close the hood. (Do not insert the grill plate.)
3. Set it to the grill function, set the temperature on high for 8 minutes. Press the start button to begin preheating.
4. Whisk the egg yolks with the sugar, salt, milk, and quark.
   Mix in the flour and then gently fold in the egg whites.
5. When the unit beeps to signify it has preheated, open the hood and add the butter to the pot – it should sizzle and melt quickly. Pour in the batter, close the hood, and cook for 8 minutes.
6. When ready, check that the cake has sufficient risen and browned. Use a silicone spatula or other non-stick safe utensil to chop it into bite-sized pieces.
7. Transfer the quark schmarrn onto serving dishes and dust with icing sugar.
8. Serve warm with apple sauce or vanilla custard.

# CONCLUSION

I hope you will enjoy each of the new recipes in your new copy of the *Ninja Foodi Grill Cookbook*. I hope it was informative and provided you with all of the tools you need to achieve your goals, whatever they may be. Let's see how much it can help you in the kitchen!

## Benefits of Using the Ninja Foodi

*Short Preparation Times*: Each of the recipes provided will clearly indicate simple steps to assemble the ingredients for your delicious meal or snack quickly. Take the time saved and spend it with your loved ones – not slaving like so many other families.

*Foods Prepared With Fewer Fats*: You will cook with about 75% less fat, which allows you to cook much healthier meals.

*Other Benefits*:

- Multi-purpose food prep
- Leaves grill marks like an outdoor grill
- Adjustable heat levels for differen  kinds of food
- Easy to clean
- No need to defrost food before grilling

## Other Tips to Make Grilling Simple

- Consider purchasing a mandolin, a unique cutting tool. You can slice, julienne, and dice veggies easily every time. Use caution and cut slowly, so you don't include your finger in the recipe!
- If a recipe calls for unchilled/room temperature eggs or butter, it is a vital step in the process, so be sure to follow the suggestions.
- It is essential to let the cooked food 'rest' a few minutes before serving to help the flavor meld. If it's meat - it will be easier to slice.
- Before serving, always taste the food, so you're sure not to over-salt or over-sweeten it.
- Chile peppers are very hot, so if you do not like 'super-hot,' discard the seeds before you begin your recipe.
- Be sure to use a pair of rubber gloves when cooking with chili peppers. Some people will cover their hands in vegetable oil and wash them with soap and water promptly after handling the hot peppers.
- If you cannot stand the nasty odor left on your hands after chopping garlic, the pros claim you can rub your fingers across something that is stainless steel, such as a spoon.

You will find this superb indoor grilling machine a welcomed addition to your kitchen.

In conclusion, please feel free to make a short review on Amazon if you have a moment or two. It is always appreciated!

Printed in Great Britain
by Amazon

15301898R00120